THE GIRL WHO MARRIED THE MOON

THE GIRL WHO MARRIED THE MOON

TALES FROM NATIVE NORTH AMERICA

TOLD BY JOSEPH BRUCHAC AND GAYLE ROSS

BridgeWater Books

To my grandmothers—J.B.

For my grandmother Ann Ross Piburn,
for my mother Elizabeth Collins,
and most especially, for my
daughter Sarah Holt—G.R.

Library of Congress Cataloging-in-Publication Data
Bruchac, Joseph, (date)
The girl who married the Moon: stories from Native North America /
told by Joseph Bruchac and Gayle Ross.
p. cm.
Includes bibliographical references.
ISBN 0-8167-3480-1 (lib.)   ISBN 0-8167-3481-X (pbk.)
1. Indians of North America—Legends.   2. Indian women—North
America—Folklore.   3. Legends—North America.
I. Ross, Gayle, (date).   II. Title.
E98.F6R68   1994   398.2'08997—dc20   93-43824

Text copyright © 1994 by Joseph Bruchac and Gayle Ross.

Illustrations copyright © 1994 by S. S. Burrus.

Designed by Leslie Bauman.

Published by BridgeWater Books, an imprint of Troll Associates, Inc.

Printed in the United States of America.

10 9 8 7 6 5 4 3 2 1

CONTENTS

INTRODUCTION

Several years ago, when Cherokee assistant chief Wilma Mankiller became principal chief of the Nation, filling the unexpired term of Chief Ross Swimmer, who had been appointed head of the Bureau of Indian Affairs in Washington, she became the object of a great deal of national attention. The media hailed her as the "first woman chief of a major American tribe." With gentle amusement, Chief Mankiller pointed out that her occupancy of this high office represented "a return to old traditional ways." Indeed, early British officials in the Southeast called the Cherokee "the Indians with the petticoat government" because of the number of women in positions of power.

Of all the misconceptions and misunderstandings perpetuated about Native peoples, the role of women in traditional cultures is perhaps the most falsely portrayed. The image of the overworked "squaw" has permeated popular books, movies, and television until the non-Native observer can be forgiven for believing that Native cultures viewed women as property to be bought, sold, or traded. Nothing could be further from the truth. Though the survival of the tribe often sharply defined the roles of both men and women, the balance that existed between the sexes was as important as the

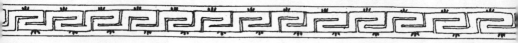

harmony between the people and the world in which they lived.

In the great matriarchal societies of the Iroquois, the ultimate power over most aspects of daily life rested with the council of Clan Mothers. In the agricultural societies of the Southwest, women wielded great economic power as the owners of the seeds, the keepers of life. Even among the western Plains peoples, with their strong warrior traditions, women were treated with love and respect. The gifts given by a suitor to a young woman's father were intended to show that the young man respected the great value of the woman to her family, and that he understood what her loss would mean to them. Though women's roles varied widely from tribe to tribe, among all Native cultures no force was considered more sacred or more powerful than the ability to create new life.

Just as a young boy must make his rite of passage into manhood, so comes the day in the life of a young girl when her body tells her she is growing into a woman. Throughout time in Native North America, that day has been celebrated with song and dance, story and ritual.

In this collection, Joseph Bruchac and I have organized the stories into four sections, reflecting the significance of the number four to Native peoples: There are four seasons, four winds, four directions, four stages in a person's life. And so we have four stories from four nations from four different regions of Native North America. Some are ancient stories that speak of the paths from youth to maturity, from foolishness to wisdom, from selfishness to caring. Two are stories of actual ceremonies that are held to celebrate a young girl's entrance into womanhood. Like human beings themselves, the stories can be beautiful or powerful, sometimes humorous, sometimes frightening. Though times change, and people and societies change with them, the wisdom of the traditional tale is everlasting.

Like Joe, I believe that now, when it has become increasingly apparent that we must find a balance between our technological society and the resources of the planet on which we live, these traditional Native tales have much to teach us. And so we offer these stories both to honor the generations of grandmothers who have gone before us and to reach the daughters and granddaughters who will come after. In the teachings of Native peoples, to speak of becoming a woman is to remember the Earth who is the mother of us all.

Gayle Ross

THE NORTHEAST

It is especially appropriate to begin this book with stories from the Northeast, for it was in this part of the North American continent that the strong roles women played in Native life were made clearest to the Europeans who arrived there as colonists in the seventeenth century. Although the most common roles of Native women were as heads of families and owners of households, numerous European visitors to the tribal nations of the New England coast also make mention of women who were chiefs and war leaders.

The five nations of the Iroquois—the Seneca, Cayuga, Oneida, Onondaga, and Mohawk—are a society divided into hereditary clans headed by women. As leaders of those clans, the women not only pass their lineage on to their sons and daughters, but they own the houses and control agriculture, too. They are also the ones who choose the chiefs and can depose a chief who fails to follow the will of the people. The Abenaki, Passamaquoddy, and Mohegans, neighbors to the east and southeast of the Iroquois, rely traditionally on the counsel of women elders and, in some cases, even have women chiefs.

Just as there were Medicine Societies for the men of the tribal nations of the northeastern woodlands, there were special women's societies that no man could belong to,

such as the Society of Women Planters among the Iroquois. This society was responsible for the extensive gardens in each Iroquois village and had special songs and ceremonies that accompanied the planting, hoeing, and harvesting of the Three Sisters—corn, beans, and squash.

When a man married, he went to live with the family of his wife. If, as sometimes happened, a couple divorced, the man went back to the longhouse of his mother, and the children remained with their mother, to whose clan they belonged. Becoming a woman among the Iroquois meant that a young girl was entering a world in which she commanded not only respect but great power.

Each of the stories in this section presents a young woman who, like those women of the Iroquois clans, is aware of her central place in her nation and is capable of showing both bravery and intelligence in the face of difficulty. "Arrowhead Finger" is a tale that tells of a young woman whose physical bravery and endurance are the equal of any boy's. "The Abandoned Girl" gives a picture of a young woman who does not despair when it seems, more than once, that all is hopeless. "The Girl and the Chenoo" reminds us that not only bravery but also kindness can help a young woman overcome obstacles and even melt a heart of ice. "The Girl Who Escaped" reveals a heroine who knows her own mind and is helped by a friend to whom she has remained faithful.

Unlike such European heroines as Sleeping Beauty or Little Red Riding Hood, who need strong men to rescue them, the female Native protagonists of these traditional tales are able to initiate action. They survive their trials and make their passages into womanhood by taking control of their own destinies.

ARROWHEAD FINGER
Penobscot

Kita! Listen. Long ago, my story was out walking around and it came to a village of the people of the Dawn Land. In that village, there was a girl who knew a great deal about plants. This was in the days before corn came to the people, and so it was very important to be able to gather food from the plants of the woods and the meadows, the swamps and the streams.

This girl always knew where to find the plants that were good to eat. In the early spring, when the berries were ripe, she would go out with her sisters and her cousins to gather strawberries from the meadows. Later in the season, in the Moon of Raspberries, they would walk among the bushes to gather red fruit in their baskets of folded birch bark sewed together with spruce roots. Because this girl was the strongest and bravest, she was the one who carried a spear, in case the bears, who also thought they owned those berry patches, should try to drive the girls away.

In the autumn, when acorns and beechnuts fell from the trees, she was always there with the other girls, collecting great loads of nuts to cook and grind into flour. She knew when to go to the marshes and gather the pollen of cattails to make flour. The girl knew, too, how to wade into the water and find the tubers of the arrowroot with her bare feet. She would dig in the soft earth at the edge of the Long River and find the white roots of the wild turnip. She enjoyed gathering plants so much that the other girls laughed and gave her the name of Gatherer. And when all the other girls were tired of collecting food and went on to other things, she would continue.

But Gatherer never took more than the people needed, for her parents had taught her this and also that one should be thankful. So, whenever she gathered any plants, she thanked each plant for the gift it gave her. The older women saw this and were pleased.

"This one will do good things for our people," they said. "The plants like her. See how they bend down their branches to make it easier for her to gather from them."

One day Gatherer went off by herself to dig roots. As she dug, she walked far into the forest, away from her village near the river. Suddenly her keen eyes saw men hiding in the brush near the trail. She knew that they were Maguak warriors, enemies of her people, come from the west to raid their village. Gatherer turned to go back to her village and warn the others, but the men saw her. Fearful that she might not escape, she called out in a loud voice, loud enough for her people to hear, "Maguak, Maguak!" Then, tucking one of the roots she had been gathering into her dress, she began to run.

She did not run far. The enemy warriors caught her and covered her mouth so that she could no longer cry out. But they knew it was too late. Soon the young men of the village would arrive, and the Maguaks knew they would be outnumbered. They tied Gatherer's hands and took her with them as a captive.

They traveled fast all day. It was only because

Gatherer was such a strong runner herself that she was able to keep up with them. She knew that she did not dare fall behind. These men were angry at her, and if she could not keep up, they might kill her.

In the evening when they made their fire, the Maguaks brought their captive close to it.

"Let us see how brave this bark-eater girl is," they said. Then they held her hand close to the fire so that the tips of her fingers burned.

Gatherer was determined not to cry out. She made no sound as they put first one hand and then the other to the fire. Finally the Maguak warriors stopped.

"This one has fingers of stone like an arrowhead," their leader said. And so they began to call her by that name, Arrowhead Finger.

That night, as the warriors slept, Arrowhead Finger reached into her dress and took out the root she had gathered.

"Help me, Little One," she said, rubbing the root over her burned fingertips.

When the Maguak warriors woke the next morning and untied their captive, they were surprised to see that her burns were healed. They traveled hard again all day, crossing over the mountains. When evening came, they made their fire and held the young girl's fingers to the flames to see if this time she would cry out. Just as before, Arrowhead Finger said nothing. And when the warriors slept, she took out the root and rubbed it on her fingers, healing her burns.

In the morning, the Maguak warriors were surprised to find that their captive's burns were, once again, gone.

"Perhaps she is carrying medicine," their leader said. "See if she has something hidden in her dress."

But without their noticing it, Arrowhead Finger swallowed the root that had helped her. When the Maguaks searched her, they found nothing. "Her hands are too hard for us to hurt her," their leader said. So, that night when they made their fire, they did not hold the young girl's hands to the flames.

They traveled on for many more days and, at last, came to their own village. The people greeted them with shouts, and because it was the custom in those days for captives sometimes to be adopted, an old woman and an old man who had lost their daughter came forward.

"We will take this girl as our daughter," said the old woman.

The young man who had led the raiding party stood in the old woman's way. "No," he said, "this one spoiled our raid. We have to decide in council what to do with her."

When the council met, the leader of the raiding party told his story. He described how Arrowhead Finger warned her village and how she refused to cry out when her fingers were burned. Many of the people in the village admired her courage. The old woman and old man spoke up again and said they wished her to be their daughter. It was agreed that until a decision was reached, Arrowhead Finger would stay with those two old people.

Then the council of chiefs went into their longhouse. They talked for many days. Finally they reached a conclusion. "We will see if this one who has been captured is indeed like an arrowhead. We will make a great fire and we will place her in it."

Not everyone in the village was pleased, however. During the short time she had been there, Arrowhead Finger had begun to make friends. People saw that she was a helpful person and a hard worker. And the old man and old woman had begun to love her like a daughter. So the council of chiefs agreed they would wait for a while before burning her.

As the moons passed, Arrowhead Finger began to notice that her body was changing. The root she had swallowed had become a baby inside her.

"We must tell our chiefs that our new daughter is expecting a child," said the old woman. Her husband went and spoke to the chiefs of the village. It was decided to wait even longer before putting Arrowhead Finger into the fire.

More moons passed. Almost everyone in the village grew to like Arrowhead Finger. She worked harder than anyone, gathering food and preparing hides, gathering wood and doing the many things that made women the heart of the village. On the day her baby was born, many of the women came to see the new child.

But that night, after Arrowhead Finger fell asleep, she heard a voice calling to her. To her surprise, her newborn son was standing beside her.

"Mother," the baby said, "I am the root you gathered in the forest long ago. Because you always treated all of the plants with respect, I will help you. In two days, your enemies in this village plan to kill you. Even now they are piling wood for a great fire. You must flee."

"How can I escape?" Arrowhead Finger said.

"Ask my grandmother for help," the baby answered, indicating the old woman who had adopted Arrowhead Finger. "She loves you and will tell you what to do. But you must leave me here so that I may do my work. Although someday we will be together again, for now you must go without me." And the baby climbed back into his cradleboard and went to sleep.

Arrowhead Finger went over to the old woman and gently woke her.

"Mother," she said, "my enemies plan to burn me. You must help me escape."

"My daughter," the old woman said, "I have been thinking a long time about how to save you. You must do just as I tell you. Tomorrow when the women gather firewood, you must go with them and leave your baby here. Then go off on the path toward the east. Because your baby is here in our lodge, they will not expect you to run away. If you keep traveling always to the east, you will reach your home."

When morning came, Arrowhead Finger woke up early and cradled her baby in her arms. "Little One," she said, "thank you for all you have given me. I do not want to leave you, but I must do as you have told me. Do not forget that one day we will be together again."

Arrowhead Finger kissed her baby, placed him in the arms of the old woman, and went to join the women collecting firewood. When they were deep in the woods, she turned off toward the rising sun and found the path. As soon as she was out of sight, she began to run. She ran all day and slept inside a hollow log at night.

Although some of the men in the village realized that Arrowhead Finger had run away, she knew the woods so well that she had concealed her trail. No one was able to track her. She traveled on and on, day after day, always going toward the rising sun. At last she came to a familiar river and saw a man in a canoe. It was her own father.

"My daughter," he said as she ran up and threw her arms around him, "I have been waiting here for you. A baby came to me in my dreams last night and told me to cross the river so that I could bring you home."

Then Arrowhead Finger returned to her own village, and all the people greeted her with great joy.

Back in the Maguak village, the young men who had wished to burn Arrowhead Finger were filled with anger at her escape. They began to make plans to go on a raiding party to recapture her.

As they made their plans, the one who was going to lead the raiding party became very sick—so sick, it seemed he would die. And, one by one, all the other young men who wished to kill Arrowhead Finger became deathly ill. No one knew how to cure them. The chiefs held a council and many people spoke, but no one knew what to do until the old woman who had adopted Arrowhead Finger came forward.

"My grandson is the one who has made the young men sick," she said. "He is protecting his mother by turning her enemies' own bad thoughts against them to make them ill. His medicine power is great. You cannot defeat him. Come to my lodge. Perhaps if you ask him for mercy, he will take pity on all of you."

Everyone listened to the old woman, and it was

decided to do as she said. The chiefs of the village went to her longhouse, where they found her grandson. To their great surprise, he was no longer a small baby but had grown into a young man.

"We have come to tell you we are sorry that we abused your mother. We know you are the one whose power is making our young men sick. Do not kill them, and we will make you chief of all the village. We will be your people."

The medicine boy listened closely as those words were spoken.

"I have heard what you say," he answered. "It was my intention to kill all those young men. But now I will let them live. Go into the forest. There I will give you the medicine plants that will make them well, for I am Gwelahb'hot, and when you need medicine, you must come to me. I will not be your chief. Instead, I will remain in the forest, which will be my wigwam. I will be one of the spirits. You will not see me, but if you show respect to the plants, I will lead you to the ones that are medicine."

So it was that medicine plants were given to the people by Gwelahb'hot. And when Arrowhead Finger walked into the forest near her village, she heard the voice of her son speaking to her, leading her to the plants which could be used to cure the sicknesses that came to the people. It is his voice that all the people who seek to find medicines hear when they listen well and treat the plants with respect, just as Arrowhead Finger did long ago.

THE ABANDONED GIRL
Seneca

Hauh oneh djyadaondyus! Hear now this story! There was a girl who lived in a village close to the great river. Her name was Dancing Reed. She was almost at the age when a young woman would choose the man she wished to marry. Soon her mother would send her to the lodge of that man's mother with a gift of marriage bread. Then she would ask that the woman's son be given to her family. It was well-known who the man would be. His name was Two Feathers, and many girls had hoped that one day he might be their husband. But it was known that the mother of Two Feathers was fond of Dancing Reed and would approve no other girl.

So it was that three of the other girls decided they would get rid of Dancing Reed. If she was gone from the village, one of them would be able to take Two Feathers as a husband.

It was the time the huckleberries were ripe and groups of women would go out from the village with their berry baskets. Knowing that Dancing Reed was one of the fastest berry pickers, the three girls made their plan. Then they went to Dancing Reed.

"Sister," they said, "we have found a good place to pick berries. Come with us and we will fill our baskets."

Dancing Reed, who never thought badly of anyone, did not suspect what they intended. *"Niaweh,"* she said. "Thank you. I will gladly come with you, sisters." She followed the three other girls, who led her down to the wide river.

"We must go in this canoe over to the big island, the one that is so far out on the river it can hardly be seen," one of the girls told her. "No one goes over there, and it has many berry bushes."

"My parents have told me it is dangerous to go to that island," Dancing Reed said. "They say Sagowenota, a powerful wizard who drowns people, lives there. They told me that he is the enemy of the Underwater People, the ones who help human beings."

"We do not believe such stories," said another of the girls, laughing at Dancing Reed's words.

"Are you afraid to go with us because of those old made-up stories?" asked the third girl.

"No," Dancing Reed said, "I am not afraid. I will go with you. I will get my things."

Then Dancing Reed ran back to her longhouse to get her berry basket. She also took with her a pouch of tobacco, for her parents had told her that the Underwater People liked it. If ever she were in trouble, she could offer tobacco to them and ask for help.

The four girls climbed into the canoe and paddled to the island. The current was very swift. It was clear that no one could swim across the river without being carried away and washed over the falls downstream. But the girls paddled hard and well, and they came to the island safely.

As soon as they pulled their boat onto the beach, they picked up their berry baskets and started to walk inland. They had gone only a short distance when Dancing Reed stopped.

"Look," she said. "There are many bushes covered with ripe berries here. This is close to the canoe. We will not have to carry our baskets so far."

"That is good," said another girl. "You stay and pick from these bushes. We will walk farther inland and find other places to pick." Then they walked up the trail and disappeared from sight.

Dancing Reed began to pick the huckleberries. Her berry basket was large, and the sun moved across the sky as she picked. When she had finished filling her basket it was late in the day, but the other girls had not returned on the trail.

Perhaps they have gone to the shore by another path, and they are waiting for me, Dancing Reed thought. She lifted the basket to her back, put her carrying strap across her forehead, and began to walk. The path led straight to the water's edge, but when she arrived there, Dancing Reed looked around in confusion.

"Have I followed the wrong path?" she said to herself. "I do not see the canoe."

She put down her berry basket and walked to the edge of the shore. Before long her sharp eyes found the marks where the canoe had been drawn back into the water, and there, in the sand, ending at the water's edge were the footprints of the other girls. They had left her on the island.

It was growing dark now and Dancing Reed looked around. Although she was in great trouble, she did not despair. Her thoughts were clear. Perhaps the wizard Sagowenota did live on this island. If she made a fire, it would lead him to her and he would drown her. She took out her pouch of tobacco and placed some next to the water.

"Underwater People," she said, "I am in need of help."

But there was no answer from the river. Dancing Reed stepped back. Her only chance was to hide. She took the basket of berries and concealed it in some bushes. Then she searched for a hiding place. Just as the sun was setting, she saw a big hollow log that had washed high up on the shore. She gathered dry moss to make a bed for herself and crawled into the log. Dancing Reed listened for a long time to the sounds of the night, fearful that she would hear the footsteps of Sagowenota. Finally, though, she fell asleep.

Dancing Reed did not know how long she slept before a loud whooping call woke her. She sat up and listened. The call came again, not from the island but from far out on the river.

Perhaps someone has come to look for me, she thought. She looked out the end of the log and saw first one light and then another and another, dancing back and forth on the river's surface. They moved as quickly as giant fireflies and were coming closer and closer.

Dancing Reed had heard that when people saw lights over the river at night, those lights were the Underwater People. Although her parents had told her those under-water beings were helpful, she also remembered that others said they could be dangerous. Dancing Reed decided it would be wisest for her to remain hidden in the log.

The lights came darting closer and closer. Then, as they reached the shore, they went out. There was no moon and so it was hard for Dancing Reed to see. But it seemed as if large shapes were sitting on the beach not far from her hiding place. They did not quite look like human beings, and Dancing Reed kept very quiet.

Then she heard the voices of the Underwater People.

"Brothers," a growling voice said, "the girl is hidden in the log."

"She will be safe tonight from Sagowenota," said another voice, softer than the first one. "He does not know she is on the island, and he will not come here while we are in council."

"It is right that we should help her," said a third voice, as harsh as flint. "I will show myself to her tomorrow and carry her back to shore."

"No, brother," said a fourth voice, which whispered like wind through a feather. "All of you are frightening to look at. If she were to see any of you, she would run away. I will show myself to her when the dawn comes and help her return to her people."

"That is good," said the first voice. "Now the girl must sleep while we have our council."

With those words, Dancing Reed found herself growing very weary. I will rest for just a moment, she thought. She closed her eyes and leaned back onto the moss. When she opened her eyes again, the bright light of early dawn was shining in through the end of the hollow log.

Dancing Reed crawled out of the log, eager to see who had offered to help her. There, at the edge of the water, she saw a sight both frightening and beautiful. A great serpent, his head lifted high, looked directly at her with his bright golden eyes. On top of his head were two big horns like those of a buffalo.

"Granddaughter," the great serpent said in his feathery voice, "I have come to help you. I am Djodi'kwado, one of the Underwater People. I have been chosen to help you escape from this island and the monster Sagowenota. You must be brave and do as I tell you."

"Grandfather," Dancing Reed said, "tell me what I must do to escape."

"You must cut twelve willow switches," Djodi'kwado said. "When I grow tired as I carry you, use one of those willows to encourage me by striking it against my side. The Thunder Beings who are summoned by Sagowenota do not like those of us who live underwater. They are not your enemies, but they will try to kill me with their lightning arrows. If I am struck by their bolts, you may also be injured. So it is important that I continue to swim quickly."

"I will do as you say, Grandfather," said Dancing Reed. She went and gathered twelve willow switches, sticking them under her belt. Then the great serpent leaned down his head.

"Quick," he said. "Sagowenota is coming to the beach."

Dancing Reed climbed up onto Djodi'kwado's neck, holding on to his horns as he lifted her up, turned, and plunged into the swift water of the river. Behind her she heard the roar of Sagowenota as he ran down the beach—too late to catch her.

"We must hurry," the great serpent said. "Sagowenota cannot reach us now, but he will surely call my enemies, the Thunder Beings!"

Djodi'kwado swam swiftly. Soon the island was left far behind. Dancing Reed looked up into the sky as the great serpent swam. Off on the western horizon, she saw a small cloud. She took up the first willow switch and began to strike Djodi'kwado's side.

"Do not slow down," she said. "The Thunder Beings are coming from the west."

As the great serpent swam on and on, the clouds grew darker and came closer. Each time he began to tire, Dancing Reed would use a willow switch to urge him on. One by one Dancing Reed used the willow switches. When the last one broke, they were still far from the shore. The sound of thunder was rumbling above them.

"Go faster," Dancing Reed shouted. "Do not stop."

"I must dive for my life, Granddaughter," Djodi'kwado cried.

Suddenly a great bolt of lightning struck the water behind them. Heavy, blinding rain fell around them. The great serpent dived down and Dancing Reed found herself struggling alone in the water. Once again it seemed that all was lost. But though she could not see the shore, Dancing Reed did not give up. She started to swim. When she had gone only a few strokes, her feet touched the bottom. She stood up just as the rain stopped. Dancing Reed could see she was not far from shore. The storm clouds drifted away and the sky became clear again. In her hand was a small piece of the great serpent's horn.

Dancing Reed walked into the village. As soon as they saw her, the three girls who had abandoned her on the island fled. They knew they were disgraced. They left the village and were never seen again.

Dancing Reed walked toward the end of the village

where she heard the sound of mourning. "What is wrong?" she said to the people standing around the longhouse of Two Feathers.

"It is the young man inside," they said. "The girl he was to marry drowned. When her three friends told him, he fell to the ground and stopped breathing."

"Look at me," she said. "I am Dancing Reed. I have not drowned."

"Then you have come too late," an old man said. "Nothing can be done. Two Feathers is dead."

"No," said Dancing Reed, "I will not give up now."

Dancing Reed went into the longhouse. The people inside turned to look at her with surprise, but no one spoke, for she held the piece of the great serpent's horn in her hand. Everyone knew that such a gift from the Underwater People gave special power to the one who held it. She went straight to the place where Two Feathers lay. His face was pale and his skin was cold. She placed the piece of horn on his chest, and he began to breathe again. The color returned to his face and he sat up.

"Dancing Reed," he said. "I had a terrible dream. I dreamed that you had drowned."

The next day, Dancing Reed's mother made marriage bread for her. When Dancing Reed took it to the mother of Two Feathers, the older woman gladly gave her son to the fine young woman who had saved his life.

So it was that Dancing Reed and Two Feathers were married and lived together in happiness. And as long as she lived, Dancing Reed always remembered to leave gifts of tobacco on the shore for the Underwater People.

Naho. Here this story ends.

THE GIRL AND THE CHENOO
Passamaquoddy

Long ago, there was a girl whose older brothers were hunters. When they went on their hunting trips far into the forest, she would sometimes go with them. Because she was always ready to hear their stories, they called her Little Listener and were happy to have her along. As she was the youngest, Little Listener was usually the one chosen to stay behind and take care of their camp. While her brothers were out on the game trails, she would repair their bark-covered lodge, gather plants for food and dry wood for their fire. Then, near the end of the day, she would cook their meal in the big pot.

Each night, when her three brothers returned from their hunting, they would all sit around the fire and speak of what had happened to them that day. They often had exciting stories to tell.

"Today," her oldest brother might say, "I found the tracks of a great moose and followed them across the hills. At last I caught up with the moose by the fork in the crooked stream. But when I saw how big it was, I knew that if I killed it, it would be hard to carry its meat and hide back to our camp. And I already had caught enough game for the day. So I let it go."

"Today," her second brother might say, "I found the den of a big bear. Just as I looked inside for it, I heard a sound behind me. There was that bear! But when I saw it was a mother with cubs, I knew it would not be right to shoot it. I had to run for my life to escape."

"Today," her third brother, who was the most imaginative of the three, might say, "I was on the track of two deer. I had one arrow, so I waited until they were standing right next to each other. When I shot, my arrow went through the first deer and also killed the second one. Why have I brought home only one deer? After I put down my bow, a great mountain lion dropped from a tree branch. I picked up a stick and fought for a long time. See this scratch here on my hand? When it saw it could not defeat me, it grabbed the bigger deer and ran off."

So the three brothers would brag about their day of hunting. And whenever they asked their sister what she had done, her answer was always the same.

"My day was quiet," Little Listener would say. "I gathered food plants and firewood, and I cooked our meal."

It went on that way for some time. Then one night when the brothers returned, all three of them seemed to be badly frightened.

"I have seen strange tracks to the north," the first brother said. "Like those of a man, but much larger."

"I have also seen those tracks," said the second brother. "But I saw them to the west."

"I have seen such tracks, too," said the third brother. "I found those tracks to the south."

"I have seen nothing strange," said the girl. "I have gathered berries and firewood, and I have made our meal."

That night, as they sat around the fire, the three brothers were quiet. At last the oldest brother spoke. "Brothers," he said, "I think we were mistaken. I think those were only the tracks of bears."

The two other brothers quickly agreed with him. Their young sister, however, remained silent. She, too, had actually seen such tracks. They had been very close to the eastern edge of the hill by their camp. And Little Listener knew those tracks were not those of a bear. There was only one creature that could make such tracks. It was the Chenoo, the great cannibal monster in the shape of a man. But she knew that even to speak the name of the Chenoo would invite it into their camp. So she said nothing as her brothers spoke, laughing and joking about being frightened by mere bear tracks.

The next morning the three brothers set out to hunt as usual, leaving their sister behind to care for the camp. But Little Listener did not do her daily chores. Instead she cooked up a big pot of venison stew and placed it in the center of their lodge. She propped open the door of the lodge and spread bearskin robes to the left of the door to make a place of honor for a guest. Then she sat and listened and waited. Before long she heard the sound of heavy feet walking around the camp. Although they came closer and closer up the hill toward the wigwam, Little Listener did not move. Now the footsteps were so close that the lodge shook with each step. Still Little Listener did not move or speak. The footsteps stopped, and she could see the big shadow of someone standing just outside the door. That was when Little Listener spoke.

"Grandfather," she said, "I am glad you have come to visit me. Come inside. I have cooked a special meal for you."

As soon as she spoke, the huge head and shoulders of the Chenoo filled the door of the lodge.

"Granddaughter," the monster said, his voice like the rumbling of great boulders rolling down a hill, "I accept your invitation."

Then the Chenoo squeezed his way into the wigwam. Even though the lodge was large enough for Little Listener and her three brothers, the Chenoo barely fit inside. His big shoulders pressed against the sides of the wigwam, and his head reached up to the smoke hole in the roof.

"Grandfather," Little Listener said, pushing the bowl of stew toward the Chenoo, "I know you are hungry. This food is for you to eat."

The Chenoo reached out one hand and picked up the big clay stewpot as if it were a small drinking cup. He swallowed the stew with one gulp and then smiled, showing teeth as large as spearpoints.

"Granddaughter," the Chenoo rumbled, "I am glad you greeted me and invited me inside. I was about to eat you. But as I have learned you are my relative, I will not hurt you or the others who live in this lodge. Tell me what I can do to help you."

"Grandfather," Little Listener said, "I am glad you have recognized me. There may indeed be some things that you can do to help. Now, though, all I want you to do is rest. I know you must be tired from walking so far to the north and the east, the south and the west. I have made a place for you with those bear robes. Go to sleep."

The Chenoo smiled again. "Granddaughter, I am tired indeed. I will do as you say and I will rest." Then the Chenoo lay down on the bear robes, covering the entire floor of the wigwam, and fell asleep.

Little Listener went outside. She closed the door of the lodge and sat in front of it with a smile on her face.

That evening, when her brothers returned, they were happy and full of stories.

"Today I have hunted well. Look at these rabbits I have brought back," said the oldest brother.

"Today I, too, have hunted well. See the fine goose I have here," said the second one.

"Today," said the third brother, "I have brought home this fine deer that I killed with one arrow."

Little Listener sat smiling in front of the closed door of the lodge, saying nothing. At last, when the three brothers had finished telling their stories, they asked her what she had done that day.

"My day was quiet," she said. "I gathered berries and gathered firewood. I made a big stew and invited our grandfather into our lodge."

"Our grandfather is here?" said the three brothers.

"Indeed," said Little Listener. "He is sleeping now. I will wake him, but you must promise me to greet him as your relative when he comes outside."

"Of course we will greet him," her brothers said. "Wake him up."

Then Little Listener pulled open the door of the wigwam.

"Grandfather," she said, "your other grandchildren are here. They wish to greet you."

As soon as she spoke, the Chenoo poked his huge head and shoulders out of the lodge. The three brothers stared at him, so frightened they could not speak.

"Greet your grandfather," Little Listener said.

The three older brothers spoke in shaking voices. "Grandfather," they said, "we welcome you. We are glad to see you. It has been so long since we have seen you that you appear new to us."

The Chenoo came out of the lodge and stood to look down at them. "Grandsons," he said, "I am glad you have greeted me as a relative." He looked at the game they had brought back. "I see you have gotten food for my dinner."

Then the Chenoo reached out and swallowed the rabbits and the goose with one gulp and the deer with another. The three brothers simply sat and stared.

"Grandfather," Little Listener said, "now that you have eaten, we have nothing for our own meal. Can you bring us some food?"

"Whatever you ask, I will do," said the Chenoo. He took four big strides. The first carried him out of the camp. The second carried him down the hill. The third carried him across the valley, and the fourth carried him out of sight.

"Brothers," Little Listener said, "try to remember to be more friendly to our grandfather when he returns."

No sooner had she finished speaking than the Chenoo came striding back into camp, carrying two huge moose, one in each hand.

From that point on, life was easy for Little Listener and her brothers. The Chenoo made a lodge for himself from big trees and camped close to them. Each day he helped them with their hunting. Not only were they able to feed themselves and the Chenoo on the game he brought, they also got many skins for trade and dried much meat to share with their relatives in the village.

When the time came for them to return, Little Listener went to say good-bye to her grandfather.

"We must return to our people," she said to him.

"Granddaughter," said the Chenoo, "I wish to come with you. But I do not wish to frighten the people. Although I may not appear fearsome to you and my grandsons, some people may be afraid of the way I look. Will you help me?"

"Yes, Grandfather. Tell me what we must do."

"Make for me a sweat lodge and make it very hot."

So Little Listener and her three brothers made a big sweat lodge. When it was ready, the Chenoo went inside by himself and they closed the door of the lodge. After he had been there awhile, he called to Little Listener, "It is not hot enough."

Little Listener opened the door, and her brothers piled on more hot stones. The red-hot stones were higher than the height of a tall man, but still the Chenoo called for heat. Three more times they opened the door and brought more stones. Then the Chenoo stayed inside a long, long time. At last Little Listener called in to him.

"Grandfather," she said, "are you all right?"

The voice that answered was small and weak. "Open the door, Granddaughter," it said. "I am ready."

When Little Listener opened the door, out crawled not the giant Chenoo but an old man, no larger than any other old man. His hair was long and white, and his face was kind. He leaned over and coughed. Out of his mouth came a piece of ice shaped like a man.

"Granddaughter," he said, "that is my heart. Throw it

into the fire, and I will be able to remain a human being as you see me now."

Her three brothers were afraid to touch it, but Little Listener grabbed the icy heart of the Chenoo and threw it into the fire. It melted away.

So it was that the kindness of Little Listener melted the heart of the giant Chenoo. So it was that she and her three brothers brought their grandfather back to the people. And when I last visited their village, all of them were still living there in happiness.

THE GIRL WHO ESCAPED
Mohegan

There was once a girl named Flying Bird. She liked nothing better than to play in the forest with the dolls she made of wood and cornstalks. Her mother sometimes scolded her for not playing with the other children. But Flying Bird still preferred to go alone into the woods.

One day, as she was playing, Flying Bird noticed that she was not alone. A very small woman, no taller than her knee, was watching her from behind some berry bushes.

"Come and play with me," Flying Bird said.

The little woman joined her and the two of them played. From that time on, Flying Bird would come each day to visit with her new friend in the woods. She never said a word about it, for it was said that if you ever told anyone you had met one of the Makiawisag, the Little People, you would never see one of those Little People again.

Flying Bird grew to love her little friend. Whenever she ate a meal, Flying Bird would always take a bit of food and place it outside the lodge on a piece of bark so that Makiawisqua could share it with her.

"My friend," Makiawisqua told her one day, "whenever you are in trouble, you can use your dolls to call on me to help you. Just talk to one of them, and I will hear it as clearly as if I were there."

As Flying Bird grew older, she turned from a little girl into a strong young woman. However, she always carried at least one of her dolls under her belt as a way of keeping her friend Makiawisqua with her.

Now it was the time a young woman might choose a husband, but Flying Bird continued to prefer spending time by herself in the woods. Some of her friends teased her about this.

"Do you have a secret husband who is a bear?" they would say. And then everyone, including Flying Bird, would laugh. Because she was good-natured and friendly, Flying Bird was very popular. Her parents knew that she was a strong-minded young woman and would eventually find a young man to her liking. So they did not try to force her into marriage. Only a fine young man would be good enough for their daughter.

One day a middle-aged man came to the village. Although he spoke their language and said he was a Mohegan, no one had ever seen him before. His name was Rough Hands. He explained that his village was far removed from the place where Flying Bird and her people lived, a journey of many days to the west of the Long River. Still, the people welcomed him. They gave him food and a place to stay in one of their lodges.

That night, as everyone sat around the fire, he stared at Flying Bird. "I would like to take this young woman for a wife," Rough Hands said.

His words did not make Flying Bird happy. This strange man did not act in a friendly way. And there was something in his eyes she did not like.

"I am not yet ready to take a husband," Flying Bird said.

"You will not find a better husband than I," said Rough Hands. "I am a great hunter and have more power than anyone in this village."

The people of Flying Bird's village did not like such words. But Flying Bird's mother answered Rough Hands politely, saying "Our daughter is not yet ready to leave her home."

A dark cloud seemed to pass over the strange man's face, but he said nothing more. That night Rough Hands waited until all the people in the village had gone to their lodges. He began to sing a magical song. The song had so much power that everyone fell fast asleep. Then he crept into the lodge where Flying Bird and her family were sleeping. He took out a cord and tied it tightly around Flying Bird's hands and feet, picked her up, and carried her off.

When Flying Bird awoke, she was in a canoe going down the river. She tried to move, but her hands and feet were tied.

"You were not ready to leave your home," said a harsh, mocking voice. "Are you ready now?"

Flying Bird turned her head and saw Rough Hands, sitting in the back of the canoe with his paddle in his hand and an ugly smile on his face. She said nothing in response to his words.

All that day, as they went down the river, Flying Bird did not speak. At last, when it was growing dark, Rough Hands pulled his canoe up to the shore. He lifted out his captive.

"We will spend the night here," he said. "I have a fine shelter that I made on my way to your village."

Carrying Flying Bird over his shoulder, Rough Hands walked up the bank and to the edge of the forest. There stood a poorly made lean-to constructed of dry sticks and rotting bark. Rough Hands dumped his prisoner on the ground and threw an old deerskin blanket over her. He made a big fire before standing up and throwing a pack over his shoulder.

"I am going to check the snares I left here," he said. "When I come back, you can cook my food for me."

As Rough Hands disappeared into the forest, Flying Bird tried to free herself, but the knots were too tight. Suddenly she remembered that she had with her one of her dolls, tied to her belt by a string.

"My friend," she said, looking at the doll, "I am in trouble. Come and help me."

Something struck the side of the lodge. Something struck it again. Then Flying Bird saw a third pebble hit the side of the lean-to. When she looked up, she saw the one who threw it—her friend, Makiawisqua.

The little woman walked over to her. She touched the cords that held Flying Bird's hands and feet, and they came untied.

Flying Bird stood up, but she felt too weak to run. How could she escape before Rough Hands came back?

"Ask your friend to help us," Makiawisqua said. "Blow on the wooden doll."

Flying Bird took the wooden doll from her belt. As she blew on it, the doll grew larger and larger. Soon it was the same size as Flying Bird and looked just like her. The little woman breathed on the doll, and it began to breathe. She placed it under the old deerskin blanket, took Flying Bird by the hand, and led her far away from the camp.

When Rough Hands returned to his lean-to, he was not happy. His snares, which had been poorly made, were all empty. And the fire had burned down to a few coals.

"My wife," he said, "do not be afraid. I have come back for you." He built up the fire and was pleased to see by its light that Flying Bird was there as he had left her. But when he crawled under the blanket and put his arms around the wooden doll he thought was his captive, his arms and hands filled with splinters.

Far down the trail that led through the hills, Flying Bird and Makiawisqua heard a terrible howling sound. "That bad man has discovered you are gone. We must not stop," Makiawisqua said.

The moon had risen and its light was very bright. They looked back from a hilltop and saw Rough Hands running very fast across the valley below, following their trail.

Makiawisqua took a stone from the pouch on her belt, and said to Flying Bird, "Throw this toward that bad man."

Flying Bird took the stone and threw it toward Rough Hands, who had almost reached them. As soon as the stone struck the earth in front of the bad man's feet, it grew and grew until it was a tall range of mountains. Today all that remains of those mountains is Wintechog Hill in southwestern Connecticut.

Flying Bird and Makiawisqua began to run once more. The sun rose in the sky and still they ran. But while they raced across a wide meadow, Makiawisqua looked back. Rough Hands was close behind them.

"That bad man is getting close again," she said. The little woman reached up and took a comb made of carved bone from her hair. She handed it to Flying Bird. "Throw this down on the ground between us."

Flying Bird took the comb and hurled it to the ground. As soon as it struck, the comb turned into a field of briers and brambles that tangled around Rough Hands and held him tight. Some of those briers still grow to this day in the hills around Uncasville, near the Thames River in Connecticut.

Flying Bird and Makiawisqua began to run as before. They ran all that day, heading to the northwest toward the Long River. At last they were close to the place where Rough Hands had crossed the river. Flying Bird's village was on the other side.

"I can go no farther with you," Makiawisqua said. "Now you must take care of yourself." She took a tiny birch-bark canoe and a paddle made from a spruce twig out of her pouch. As she blew on them, they grew larger. "Go quickly," she said. "That bad man is near us again."

Flying Bird pushed her canoe out onto the wide river and began to paddle. When she was halfway across, she looked back. There was Rough Hands, close behind her in another canoe. Instead of paddling it, he was singing a magic song and the canoe was speeding across the water toward her. Just as it seemed he was about to catch up with her, on the other shore Makiawisqua began to sing a song of her own. As she sang, the currents in the river divided and began to push the boat of the bad man back toward the other shore. Flying Bird paddled as hard as she could. The current helped her, carrying her farther and farther away from Rough Hands. His song turned into howling, then stopped. When she looked around, his boat had vanished. He was never seen again.

So Flying Bird escaped from the man who tried to force her to be his wife. She returned to her village, where her parents and friends greeted her with joy.

Less than a moon later, a fine young man named Good Eyes from another Mohegan village to the south came with his parents to visit. As soon as Flying Bird saw him, she knew he was the man she wanted for a husband. As soon as he looked at her, Good Eyes knew that he wanted her for his wife. So things went very well when Flying Bird asked her mother to go to the mother of Good Eyes and speak of marriage. Within a few moons, the two young people were wed.

Flying Bird and her husband lived together happily and had strong children. It was said that of all the girls in the village, their daughters always had the best dolls. And they were never scolded by their mother for playing by themselves in the forest.

THE SOUTHEAST

The southeastern part of what is now the United States covers a vast area with diverse topography, from coastal lands to mountains to rich river valleys. Before European contact, this region was home to some of the most advanced societies found in Native North America. The people were skilled artisans, hunters, and fishermen with a complex social system. Extensive trade routes existed between nations, and most tribes possessed special skills, such as basketmaking or shell carving, producing goods that were prized by other peoples. Though many nations were often at war with their neighbors, Native warfare differed greatly from its European counterpart, consisting as it did of small-scale raids that resulted in few casualties.

Perhaps the largest and most powerful of the southeastern tribes, the Cherokee made their home in the Great Smoky Mountains in parts of North Carolina, Tennessee, Georgia, and Kentucky. To the south were the Creek, or Muskogee, people, neighbors and traditional enemies of the Cherokee. On the southwestern border of this region lived the Caddo, while the Piankeshaw, or Peoria, people were found to the north in present-day Indiana. Pressured by other tribes and the westward expansion of white settlements, the Piankeshaw moved west; first to Missouri, where the story "The Girl Who Married an

Osage," is set, and then on to Oklahoma. The majority of tribes originally from the southeast may be found today in Oklahoma, as a result of the forced migration of Native people to land west of the Mississippi River.

Like their relatives in the Northeast, women in the southeastern tribes were powerful and respected members of their societies. A young girl was considered to have begun her entrance into womanhood when she first experienced menstruation. In most Native American cultures, women having their "moontime" stayed apart from the general population, usually in a special women's lodge. Viewing the custom through prevailing Western biases, early European observers assumed women were seen as "unclean" at such times, or "sick."

On the contrary, Native people simply understood that the ability to create life is the strongest power there is, and believed that women showing physical evidence of that power could neutralize or divert any other formulas, rituals, or ceremonies being practiced. This idea is explained in the Cherokee story "Stonecoat."

The tradition of the warrior woman, very common in the Southeast, is the theme of the Creek story "The Girl Who Helped Thunder." The girl wins the friendship of Thunder, using skills commonly thought of as belonging to men. In the Piankeshaw story "The Girl Who Married an Osage," the time-honored motif of the star-crossed lovers is explored, along with the transformation resulting from a sacrifice to that love. Finally, we see the journey from childhood to maturity, from foolishness to wisdom, in the Caddo story "The Girls Who Almost Married an Owl."

STONECOAT
Cherokee

This is what the old women told me when I was a girl. Once, long ago, all the people of the settlement went out into the mountains on a great hunt. One hunter went alone, ahead of the others. He climbed to the top of a high ridge, and on the other side he found a large river. His eyes scanned the ridge across the river for game. Instead, he saw something very strange. An old man came walking along that ridge, leaning on a staff that seemed to be made of some bright shining rock. Once in a while, the old man would lift the staff and point it in a certain direction, then draw it back and smell the end of it. At last he pointed it in the direction of the people's hunting camp, and the staff seemed to glow even brighter, until it shone like the sun. This time when the old man drew back the staff, he sniffed the end of it several times as if it smelled very good. And he turned and started down the ridge, straight toward the camp of the people.

Now the hunter had never seen anything quite like this, and he did not know what to think. So he hid himself and continued to watch the old man. The old man moved very slowly, leaning on that shining staff. When he reached the edge of the ridge, he lifted the staff into the air and spoke to it. Then he hurled it as high as he could. The hunter watched in astonishment as the staff grew into a bridge of glowing rock that stretched all the way across the river. When the old man had crossed the river, he held out his hand and the bridge became a staff again. He picked it up and started over the mountain, straight for the camp of the people.

The hunter was very frightened. He felt sure that the old man meant evil for his people. So he hurried down the mountain and took the shortest trail back to the camp, in order to arrive before the old man. When he got there and told his story, the elders became alarmed. They knew at once what the hunter had seen. It was Nun-yunu-wi, Stonecoat, a wicked cannibal monster who lived in that part of the country and hunted human beings. It was hard to escape from him because his staff guided him like a good hunting dog. And it would be even harder to kill him, because his whole body was covered with a skin of solid rock. If Stonecoat found the camp, he would kill and eat them all.

The men of the camp began to arm themselves and prepared to defend the camp. But the *ada wehi*, the medicine man, stopped them, saying, "There is no stronger power than that of Stonecoat. We will have to defeat him another way. The power to bring new life is greater than the power to kill. We must speak to the women."

And so the men sought among the women for those who were in their moontime, that time when women show physical signs of their power to give birth, to create new life. They found seven women who were in that way, and they all agreed to try to use this power to save the lives of the people.

The women stood along the trail Stonecoat would

follow. They stood some distance from each other, so that the oldest was the farthest away and the youngest stood just outside the camp.

Soon they heard Stonecoat coming along the trail, and they could see the glowing rock of his staff. When he saw the first woman, he flinched and cried out, "*Yu*, my grandchild, you are in a very bad way!"

But the woman stood still and straight, and replied: "No, Grandfather, I am in a sacred way."

He hurried past her. In a moment, he met the second woman, and again he cried out: "*Yu!* Granddaughter, you are in a very bad way!"

The second woman also replied, "No, Grandfather, I am in a sacred way."

Stonecoat passed this woman, too, but now he was much weaker. He hurried on and met the third, fourth, and fifth women. With each woman he passed, his step grew slower and his voice was growing faint.

As he passed the sixth woman, blood began to trickle from his mouth and his steps began to falter. Still, he passed her and went on toward the camp. The seventh woman was a young girl who was having her very first moontime. When Stonecoat saw her, blood began to pour from his mouth and he fell down upon the trail. The medicine man hurried to him and drove seven sourwood stakes through his body, pinning him to the ground. When night came, the men piled great logs over him and set fire to them, and all the people gathered to watch.

Now Stonecoat was a great *ada wehi* and knew many secrets. As the fire began to come close to him, he spoke to the people, saying, "The sacred powers of these women have defeated me. I will teach you what I know before I die."

And so Stonecoat began to talk and to teach them the medicine for all kinds of sickness. At midnight he began to sing, and he sang the hunting songs for the deer and the mountain buffalo, and for all the animals of the forests and the mountains. As the fire grew hotter, his voice sank lower and lower, until at last, when daylight came, the fire was a pile of white ashes and the voice was still.

The people raked away the ashes. Where the body of Stonecoat had been, there was only a great crystal stone that they gave to the medicine man to use in his healing work. Where the shining staff had been was a lump of the sacred red wadi paint—its color the symbol of power and triumph.

The medicine man called the people to him and painted them on the face and chest. And whatever each person prayed for while the painting was being done— hunting success, working skill, or a long and happy life—that prayer was answered.

THE GIRL WHO HELPED THUNDER

Muskogee (Creek)

Long ago, among the Muskogee people, there lived a girl who was a very skillful hunter. When she was small, she would follow her brothers, learning first to hunt game with a blowgun, then to master the bow and arrow. Often her skill would leave older boys grumbling as she won honors in the target-shooting contests they held among themselves. But more than anything, she loved to hunt—to bring home meat to help feed her family. And she looked forward longingly to the day when her male relatives would invite her to join them in a hunting party.

At last the day came when her uncles asked her to travel with them into the mountains. When they reached the site of the hunting camp, she realized they meant for her to cook and take charge of the camp. Still, she did not complain but went about her duties as best she could.

One day, as she was preparing *sofkee,* or cornmeal mush, for the men to eat, she heard a deep rumble of thunder. Yet this thunder did not come from the sky. It seemed as though it came from the stream running next to the camp. She hurried down to the water and saw an old man struggling to free himself from the coils of a *stahwanaia,* or tie-snake, who lived in the rivers and streams. Every time the man thrashed to throw off the coils of the snake, the thunder rolled; and as the snake writhed, the girl could see a bright white spot flashing on its neck.

As soon as they saw the girl, both the snake and the old man began to call for her help. "Shoot the white spot on his neck," pleaded the old man, "or he will drown me. It is the only way to kill him."

"Shoot the old man," called the snake, "or his thunder will kill you."

At first the girl stood helplessly, unable to decide what she should do. Then she remembered that Thunder often brought rain, which helped corn to grow. So she carefully aimed her arrow at the white spot on the snake's neck and loosed it, killing the tie-snake instantly. The coils slid from around the old man's body as the snake sank into the water of the stream.

Now Thunder, for that was who the old man was, turned and walked out of the stream and over to where the girl was standing. "You are just a young girl," Thunder said, "but you will always be my friend. There is a time of trouble coming for your people. If you will listen to me and do as I say, I will give you the power to help." And Thunder told the girl exactly what she should do.

"You must purify yourself to prepare for this power," said Thunder. "You must do the medicine fast that young men do when they seek spirit guidance for their lives. In this way, you will be ready when the time comes.

"You will sing the song I am about to teach you, and great power will be yours." Then Thunder taught the girl the song and cautioned her not to use it unless her people were in danger.

When the uncles returned to camp, they packed up and made ready to return to the village. On the trail, the girl walked behind her uncles as Thunder had told her to do. Along the way, she asked each of her uncles to help her undergo a four-day medicine fast. Three times she asked, but the older uncles said, "There is no use in that. You are too young."

Finally the fourth and youngest uncle said, "Since you have asked, I feel I must help you." And when they reached the village, the youngest uncle kept his promise. He made all the arrangements for the ceremony, just as he would have for a nephew. He helped the girl as an uncle should.

He stayed with her through the long night in the sweathouse. Then he took her to a secluded place where she would remain alone for the four days of fasting. As the girl prayed during her long vigil, the words of Thunder came back to her: "I will give you the power to help."

In the fall of that year, when most of the men were away hunting to provide meat for the coming winter, word reached the village that a great party of Cherokee warriors was making its way from the north. As the war party approached the village, the youngest uncle of the Girl Who Helped Thunder went looking for her. He had seen her skill with weapons, and he wanted her to fight with him. Drawing near to her home, he saw her walking away from the village, going toward the east. He followed her and watched as she walked around the village in a great circle, singing in a language he had never heard before. Four times she circled her people; four times she sang the song. When he saw her again, she had taken the shape of a brilliant rainbow.

The Cherokee, too, noticed the beautiful rainbow, arcing over their heads. From high above, the Girl Who Helped Thunder lifted her bow and began firing white-hot bolts of lightning. Thunder rolled as her arrows exploded at the foot of the enemy.

When all the Cherokee warriors were dead or captured, the Girl who Helped Thunder took back her own shape. She spoke to her captives, saying, "Return to your people and tell them what happened here." In fear and confusion, the Cherokee retreated from that village and they did not return.

And to this day the story is told of how the Girl Who Helped Thunder used the sacred power given her to save the lives of her people.

THE GIRL WHO MARRIED AN OSAGE
Piankeshaw (Peoria)

The long winter had ended. The Piankeshaw people in the village led by Chief Sauk-ton-qua were preparing to leave their winter camp in the Bois Brûlé to return to the summer hunting grounds in the west. The women sang as they worked, and the men's hearts were light. Warm weather was coming, bringing the season of plenty.

But for Mina-Sauk, the daughter of Chief Sauk-ton-qua, the approach of spring brought no joy. With worried eyes, the chief watched his daughter. He saw how pale and listless she had become; he saw the pain in her eyes. Mina-Sauk had been ill all winter. Neither the loving care of her family nor the cures of the medicine men had been able to help her. Mina-Sauk's sickness was not of the body, but of the heart.

In the hunting season of the year before, Mina-Sauk had been captured by a raiding party of the Osage, longtime enemies of the Piankeshaw. For four months, she lived in an Osage village far to the north. There she fell in love with an Osage warrior and married him. When she was retaken by the warriors of her father, her homecoming was not a joyous one, for she grieved at the loss of her mate. Not even the words of her father or the pleadings of her mother could make Mina-Sauk forget her husband.

"No happiness can come of this marriage," the old chief told his daughter. "Has the love of this Osage caused you to forget your people?"

"I have not forgotten my people," Mina-Sauk replied, "but I cannot forget the love I feel for my husband. Manitou, the maker of all things, put this love in my heart. Only Manitou can remove it."

The summer camp of this band of Piankeshaw people was nestled on the side of a mountain that fell away in three steep granite ledges. It was a place easy to defend, even with many men out in hunting parties. Near the end of June, the Moon When Flowers Bloomed, women returning from the stream on the valley floor hurried to find Chief Sauk-ton-qua. They had seen Mina-Sauk at the water. She was with her Osage husband. Now that winter's grip on the land was broken, he had traveled from his home in the north to find his wife and take her away with him. Quickly Sauk-ton-qua sent his warriors to capture this Osage and bring him to the village.

The people of Sauk-ton-qua gathered around a council fire that night. In their midst was the Osage husband, a prisoner, tightly bound. For many hours, the people spoke what was in their hearts, and Sauk-ton-qua and his elders listened. Men spoke of the children they had lost to Osage raiding parties, and women talked of husbands lost in the Osage wars.

At last the medicine man spoke, saying, "The power of this Osage man makes a prisoner of Mina-Sauk. He is an enemy and he should die like one. Mina-Sauk will then be free and her heart will heal."

When she heard these words, Mina-Sauk could no

longer be silent. In anger and in grief, she spoke to the people, saying, "Manitou put this love in my heart. Destroy my husband and you will destroy me. You will destroy yourselves."

But hate for the Osage had hardened the people's hearts against her, and they would not listen.

Sauk-ton-qua sent men to stand on the granite ledges. The Osage husband was pushed from the side of the mountain. When his body landed on the first ledge, the men waiting there threw him to the second ledge, and the men there sent his broken body into the deep ravine below. A hoarse cry broke from Mina-Sauk. Struggling free from the arms of the women, she leaped from the edge of the cliff to join her husband in death. Her mangled body landed at the bottom of the ravine, next to that of the man she loved.

As the people watched in horror, a great bolt of lightning split the sky and the voice of Thunder spoke. The side of the mountain exploded, killing the people of Sauk-ton-qua. A great storm raged. Then, as suddenly as it had come, it was gone. Where the lightning had struck, the earth was split and a stream of water, the tears of Mina-Sauk, poured down over the granite ledges, washing everything clean. In the ravine at the foot of the falls, where the blood of Mina-Sauk pooled with that of her husband, bright red flowers were growing. Now called Indian pinks, they bloom each year in the Flower Moon at the foot of Mina-Sauk Falls.

THE GIRLS WHO
ALMOST MARRIED AN OWL
Caddo

One time there lived a man and woman who were married for many years, yet no babies were born to them. Finally, when the woman was almost past the age of childbearing, twin daughters came. The couple was overjoyed. They named the firstborn First Daughter; and the second twin was called Little Sister.

As the girls grew, they were so much alike that only their parents could tell them apart, and they were as close as two sisters could be. When the time came for them to marry, the old couple arranged a visit with the family of first one man and then another. But First Daughter and Little Sister always refused these men, saying, "We do not want to be separated; we want to share a husband. Therefore, the man we marry must be wealthy enough to take care of us both."

At last the twins heard of a great chief from a faraway village. Rumors of his wealth and his fame as a leader had spread throughout the country. "This man would make a fine husband," First Daughter told her twin, and Little Sister agreed. So the girls went to their parents to ask permission to seek the village of this chief, in order to offer themselves in marriage. Now this made the old couple very sad, for they were too old to undertake such a journey. If this chief accepted the twins, the old people might never see their grandchildren. Still, they could not find it in their hearts to refuse their daughters.

First Daughter and Little Sister worked very hard to prepare for the journey. The old woman made beautiful dresses of white buckskin for the girls to wear, and their father dried meat for their traveling food. Finally all was ready, and the twins bade their parents farewell and set out in search of the wealthy chief.

When the girls camped that night, they began to talk about the powerful chief they hoped to marry. "Of course, he will be a good man," First Daughter told her sister. "He must be, or so many people would not speak of him."

"But how will we find him?" asked Little Sister. "We do not even know where his village is."

"Oh, that is easy," replied First Daughter. "So many people know of him, we can ask the first person we meet to direct us."

Neither of the twins noticed the great owl perched in the treetop, watching and listening to them talk. The next day, as they resumed their journey, the first person they met coming toward them was a young man, carrying a turkey in his hand. First Daughter and Little Sister stopped the man and began to talk to him, asking about the wealthy chief. "We want to marry him," explained First Daughter, "for we hear that he is very wealthy."

"Yet we do not know how to find his village," added Little Sister, "because we have never been there. We have not seen this man but have heard only good talk about him."

The young man grinned broadly and said, "Well, this is

good fortune! You are speaking to the very chief you seek, and I live just a little way from here. I am on my way home after attending a very important council. I would be glad to marry both of you. Wait here while I run home and speak to my grandmother about this." The twins thought it was very strange that such a powerful chief should have to tell his grandmother, but they said nothing.

The young man, who was none other than Owl, ran on to his lodge and called out, "Grandmother, help me clean the lodge and put it in order. I am bringing home two girls I am playing a joke on. They think I am a rich chief and want to marry me."

After they had cleaned the lodge—which was very dirty—Owl said, "I am going to put this turkey I have captured over my bed. When you get ready to cook, ask me which turkey you should prepare and pretend to point to one. I will say, 'No, take this one.' Then the girls will think we have many turkeys and many good things to eat."

Owl went back for the girls and led them to his lodge. First Daughter and Little Sister were pleased to see that everything was nice and neat, though the fire was so low that the lodge seemed very dark. But when they offered to gather more wood and build up the fire, Owl said, "Oh no, Grandmother likes to keep the lodge dark. Her eyes are sore."

"We can help you make an eyewash with the roots of the deer-eye flower," First Daughter offered.

"Yes," said Little Sister, "we used to make it for our father."

"Oh, maybe you can do that tomorrow," said Owl. "Right now we should eat."

Grandmother remembered what Owl had said and asked which turkey she should prepare. Owl made a great show of trying to decide. But when he handed the turkey to his grandmother, First Daughter took it, saying, "We can do that, Grandmother. You should rest."

At this, Grandmother saw that although the girls were young and a bit foolish, their hearts were good. She began to feel bad about Owl tricking them. While the twins were working, she crept near and whispered, "After we sit down to eat, watch my grandson carefully and see if you don't notice something about him."

When everything was ready, First Daughter and Little Sister sat down on either side of Owl. They watched him very closely. They saw the way his head turned from side to side as he listened to them talk. For the first time, they took a good look at his face. With sinking hearts, they realized that they had been tricked.

"You are no chief!" cried First Daughter. "You are only Owl!"

When the girls recognized him, Owl threw off his human disguise. With a great *whoosh* of wings, he sailed out the lodge and into the night.

First Daughter and Little Sister were ashamed of how they had been fooled. The next morning, they returned to their parents and told them everything that had happened. The twins listened more carefully to the old man and the old woman from that time on. Soon both had married good men and were happy; though neither married a wealthy chief. And the old man and the old woman were happiest of all, for when babies were born to the twins, the old couple had grandchildren to carry on their backs.

THE SOUTHWEST

The Southwest is a land of great beauty and stark contrasts—tall mountains near rugged canyons, lush forests giving way to arid deserts. Some of the oldest civilizations in Native North America are found here. The Oraibi pueblo of the Hopi people is one of the two oldest continuously inhabited cities in the United States. The term pueblo *comes from the Spanish word for "village" and describes the stone and adobe cities common throughout the area. The many different tribes who live in the pueblos share important characteristics. They are agricultural societies with strong traditions and deeply spiritual roots. Despite centuries of oppression, the pueblo cultures are still thriving in the Southwest.*

The arrival of the Spanish brought sweeping changes for two other tribes in this region: the Apache and the Navajo. Both were hunter-gatherer societies. With the introduction of the horse, the Apache became nomadic, ranging over a vast territory from the dusty mountains of present-day Mexico to the plains of the United States, where they hunted buffalo. The Navajo (Dine in their own language) followed a different path. Beginning with a few sheep taken in raids on early Spanish settlements, the Navajo cultivated them into vast flocks and became sheepherders. The Dine used the animals as a source of food; they also learned to spin and weave wool. Today Navajo blankets and rugs are prized for their beauty and durability.

From the pueblos, strung like a necklace along the Rio Grande valley, come two stories in this collection. The Santa Clara pueblo is the source of a cautionary Cinderella tale; "The Poor Turkey Girl" serves as a reminder that one must always keep a promise. From the pictographs at the Cochiti pueblo comes the classic story "The Girl Who Gave Birth to Water-Jar Boy." Pictographs are common throughout Native North America, and many are considered to be sacred. Their locations are kept secret and the sites carefully guarded.

In the Dine tale "The Bear Woman," a rite of passage is sent horribly astray by the actions of the girl's brothers and her husband, Coyote. When the girl responds with anger and violence, her transformation into Bear Woman is assured. "The Beauty Way—The Ceremony of White-Painted Woman" is drawn both from written accounts of the ceremony at the turn of the century and from a friend's observations of the ritual as it is held today. I send my love and gratitude to my small Apache friend, Dahazi, for allowing me to name the girl in this story after her.

THE POOR TURKEY GIRL
Santa Clara Pueblo

Long ago, in the village of Shu-finne, a mother and a father died, leaving behind a baby daughter. As was the custom, the little girl was given to her mother's sister to raise. But the aunt already had many children to feed, so she did not welcome her niece.

When the little girl was old enough, the aunt set her to work tending the turkeys. Each morning at daybreak the little girl would release the turkeys from their cages and herd them into the canyons to forage for food. Each night she brought them back and penned them again. Often she was sent to work without so much as a baked cake of ground meal for breakfast. And many times she went to sleep hungry at night. Her clothes were the patched and tattered remnants handed down from her cousins; and because of her aunt's neglect, the girl's face and hands were usually dirty, her hair tangled and unkempt. Most people in the village took no notice of her. Those who did simply called her Turkey Girl.

Perhaps because she was so starved for love and kindness at home, Turkey Girl took great care with the turkeys in her charge. She was so devoted to them that the turkeys came to care for her in return. They taught her how to find food in the mountains and canyons, and how to gather berries, piñons, and acorns. They combed her hair with their beaks and spun feathers into thread to mend her torn clothes. The turkeys taught her their language and would always gather at her call. In this way, with turkeys for her only friends, Turkey Girl grew into a young woman.

It was late summer and near the time for the Ta'Tsa'Po, a ceremony at Puye. Soon the people would celebrate the cutting of the wheat and the calling of the birds for the winter's food. Every night Turkey Girl listened to her cousins chatter as they sewed new *mantas,* or dresses, to wear for the dance. Every morning, as she drove the turkeys away from the village, she saw people cooking and preparing for the great feast. But Turkey Girl did not join in the planning for this festival. She knew she had only her torn and mended *manta* to wear. In her mind, she saw the people laughing and staring at her ugly clothes, and this she could not bear. Turkey Girl could not help wishing, however, that things were different and she could go to the plaza at Puye. Every day she talked to the turkeys about the ceremony, about the people from many villages who would gather for the dancing and for the great feast.

On the day of the festival, Turkey Girl rose at dawn and herded the turkeys away from the village. She did not want to see the people leaving for Puye, dressed in their finery. But she had gone only a little way into the canyon when the turkeys stopped and surrounded her. One of them, the oldest, spoke to her, saying, "Strike us with this juniper limb."

Turkey Girl refused. "You are my friends. I cannot hurt you!" she told them. Four times they asked this of her, and four times she refused. Finally all the turkeys flew at her face. Frightened, Turkey Girl picked up the juniper limb to beat them off.

Out from under the wing of the largest turkey fell a new and beautiful *manta* made of white cotton with intricate red embroidery. From the second turkey's wing fell a wonderful red, green, and black sash. A gleaming pair of white buckskin moccasins fell from the third. From the wings of the fourth fell bright necklaces and earrings of turquoise and shell.

Again the oldest turkey spoke, saying, "You must bathe and allow us to dress your hair. In these new and beautiful clothes, you may go to Ta'Tsa'Po at Puye. Enjoy the dancing and the feast, but do not forget us. Do not leave us in the canyon after dark."

Turkey Girl was overjoyed at these gifts and promised that she would never forget her friends. Quickly she bathed in the river and dressed in the new clothes. The turkeys combed her hair until it shone long and black. With her glowing face and the bright light of happiness in her eyes, Turkey Girl was truly beautiful. She left the canyon to walk to Puye after promising once more to return before dark.

When she reached the plaza, Turkey Girl was astonished that no one from her village recognized her in her fine clothes, though she noticed many young men watching her admiringly. At first she was shy and found it hard to talk. But when the dancing began, she relaxed and began to enjoy herself. Soon she was having such a good time that all thoughts of the promise she had made left her mind.

She was sitting with a group of young people about her age, enjoying the rich food prepared for the feast, when she noticed that the sun was sinking behind the mountains. It would be dark in the canyons. Turkey Girl jumped to her feet and began to run, ignoring the many voices calling after her. Frightened and sorrowful, she raced to the canyon where she had left the turkeys. But the turkeys were not there. They were scattered throughout the canyon and the mountains. Although Turkey Girl called and called, they would not answer.

She ran after them, but the turkeys ran faster. Sobbing and stumbling in the growing darkness, Turkey Girl chased her birds. Soon her beautiful new moccasins were covered with dust. The brush and thorns ripped her fine *manta*; and the strands of her necklace broke, flinging the turquoise and shells into the dark.

Finally Turkey Girl was forced to return home, knowing that life with her aunt would be even harder now that she had lost the turkeys. And to this day, wild turkeys are spread throughout the mountains and the canyons. And to this day, because of Turkey Girl's broken promise, turkeys no longer trust people but flee whenever a human being comes near.

THE GIRL WHO GAVE BIRTH TO WATER-JAR BOY
Cochiti Pueblo

The courtship of Wai'oca began in the usual way. Like other young men, her suitor, Mo-kaite, would stand next to the river road and play his flute for Wai'oca as she walked to the river with all the young women to fill her water jar. There were many flute players, but for Wai'oca there was something special in Mo-kaite's song. Still, Wai'oca followed pueblo law and never looked at Mo-kaite's face, or into his eyes. To do so was to promise marriage, and Wai'oca was not yet ready for this.

For many days, Mo-kaite played his flute for Wai'oca. At last she spoke to her father about this young man. Her father went to the elders of the pueblo to ask about Mo-kaite. "He is a fine young man," the wise ones said. "A good provider with a strong heart—but he may not marry Wai'oca." The elders explained that Mo-kaite, Mountain Lion Hunter, was of the hunting clans. Wai'oca, Duck Woman, belonged to the water clans. And the two clans could not be joined. The elders' word was law.

Sadly Wai'oca obeyed the words of her father and the elders. She would not look at Mo-kaite when he came to play his flute for her as she walked to the river. His affection for her grew, however, and she came to care very deeply for him as well.

Finally, Mo-kaite sought the elders himself and asked if there was some way he could prove that he would be a good husband for Wai'oca in spite of their clans. "Can I not be tested," asked Mo-kaite, "to show that I am worthy?"

The elders went to speak to Wai'oca's father. When she heard of this, Wai'oca asked that she be tested, too. "If we do this together," she said to her father, "then the elders will know that our hearts are true and our spirits are strong. Surely the marriage will be blessed."

And so it began. On the first day, Mo-kaite was told to gather enough wood for all the elders in the pueblo, and Wai'oca was set to work sweeping the plaza with a small broom made of pine branches. They were to work without looking at or speaking to each other, and the tasks had to be completed before sundown. This they did.

The second day, Mo-kaite was sent to track and snare several small game animals through a maze of false trails laid down in the night by the other men of his clan. Wai'oca was given the task of washing the women elders' hair in the ritual way. She began by digging for the yucca root and grinding it to make soap. After the washing, she plaited each woman's hair the way the woman wanted. It was a very long day for both Wai'oca and Mo-kaite, but the tests were done.

On the third day, Mo-kaite was given a great pouch and told to fill it with birds' feathers, which were used in the ceremonial dances. He had to fill the pouch but leave the birds to fly free. Wai'oca was put to work making corn bread for all the people of the pueblo, using the ears of corn people brought her. She broke off the kernels, ground them into meal on her *metate*, and baked the bread in the outdoor ovens. Again Mo-kaite and Wai'oca were finished before dark.

The fourth day's test was both the easiest and the hardest, for it was one of patience. Mo-kaite and Wai'oca spent the day walking around the plaza in opposite directions, to the beat of the drum. They circled the plaza four times and the drums would stop. Then they would change directions and circle the other way. They were never allowed to look at or notice each other in any way. The elders watched as they walked. When the day was over, the wise ones agreed that Mo-kaite and Wai'oca could marry.

And so Wai'oca put on her ceremonial white *manta* with the sacred red and black sash. Mo-kaite dressed in his embroidered kilt, white leggings, and brown moccasins. Wai'oca walked from the east and Mo-kaite from the west until they stood together in the center of the plaza. Finally they were married.

Still, the elders could not forget their fears for this union, and they asked Mo-kaite and Wai'oca to live outside the pueblo. Mo-kaite built a small home for Wai'oca, and the couple began their life together.

In the beginning, Wai'oca and Mo-kaite were very happy. But when they tried to have children, it began to seem that the elders' fears were justified. Each time Wai'oca became pregnant, she gave birth to a baby that was sickly. Each small spirit flew with the birds before Wai'oca could even gather the baby into her arms. In his grief, Mo-kaite began spending his days with the brothers of his hunting clan. All his time was spent hunting, drying the meat, and keeping his weapons ready.

One morning Wai'oca went to the river for water. As she knelt on the riverbank, she prayed to the Pa'waa, the water spirits, to send her a strong son. She dipped her water jar, and her lower body was splashed. The Pa'waa entered her body and began a new life.

Wai'oca and Mo-kaite were overjoyed when they realized she was again carrying a child. They prayed that this baby would live.

When the time came for the baby to be born, Mo-kaite was away with his clan. So Wai'oca went in secret to her mother in the pueblo. Because Wai'oca was not allowed inside the pueblo, her mother did everything without asking the others for help. But instead of a human baby, Wai'oca gave birth to a round clay jar with two handles. It was a water jar. The water jar cried out for food. When Wai'oca heard its voice, she knew the same love any mother feels for a new baby. Still, when she picked up the water jar and held it, Wai'oca could not keep from crying, for she had wanted a son so badly. Wai'oca's mother cried with her, but her father comforted her, for he knew this could only be the result of something very magical.

Wai'oca took her water jar home. She fed it when it cried, held it, and talked to it. And she waited for Mo-kaite's return.

It was very late at night when Mo-kaite came. The water jar was sitting in a dark corner of the room. As Mo-kaite entered, he heard a small voice calling, "Father, please feed me. I am hungry."

Mo-kaite looked at the jar in amazement. He took ground meat and dropped it into the jar, and the voice stopped! When Wai'oca arose the next morning, there was Mo-kaite, sitting next to the jar, feeding it bits of meat and talking to it.

One day the voice of the water jar said, "Father, would you take me hunting with you tomorrow? I would like to learn what you know."

Mo-kaite decided that a son should learn from his father. And so the next morning he told Wai'oca that he was taking the water jar with him on a rabbit hunt. Wai'oca cried when she heard this; but she picked up the water jar and handed it to Mo-kaite.

Mo-kaite took his son, the water jar, out on the hunt. Although the other hunters jeered and laughed at him, Mo-kaite took no notice. Suddenly two rabbits leaped from the brush and raced right in front of Mo-kaite. Startled, he reached for his throwing stick. In his haste, Mo-kaite dropped the water jar. It rolled down the hill, struck a large rock, and shattered. Overcome by fear and horror, Mo-kaite sank to the earth, and the life force left his body.

From the shards of the water jar stepped a tall young man. He was dressed in white buckskin clothing and wore his long hair in braids. Inside him was a spirit strong enough for ten men. He was Wa-tyuonyi, the Water-Jar Boy.

Wa-tyuonyi carried the body of Mo-kaite back home to Wai'oca. "Mother," he said, "Mo-kaite's spirit is no longer here. He dropped the water jar that held me, and in his fear he let the life pass out of his body." Wai'oca's joy in her son mingled with her grief for Mo-kaite, and her tears fell. Together they mourned as they placed Mo-kaite's body in the rocks facing east.

When all was done, Wa-tyuonyi decided to seek the family of Mo-kaite, to tell them of their son and grandson. Leaving Wai'oca still grieving, he walked to the east, north, and south without finding any trace of his father's people. But as he walked to the west, he came upon a beautiful natural spring where the water bubbled up and formed a large pool. Stopping to drink from the water, Wa-tyuonyi saw an older man's face reflected in the water. When the young man turned to look, Mo-kaite was standing before him.

Mo-kaite took Wa-tyuonyi's hand and they walked into the pool. With the water rushing over them, they swirled around and around until they crossed the bridge to the world of the Pa'waa spirits. There Mo-kaite taught Wa-tyuonyi all that he had learned. But when Wa-tyuonyi asked about Wai'oca, Mo-kaite could only shake his head in silence. He was not allowed to speak of those who were in the outer world. And so Wa-tyuonyi returned to the world above and traveled home. When he arrived, he found that Wai'oca's grief had made her very ill. Holding her close, Wa-tyuonyi whispered the prayer he had learned from his father, for passing on to the other place. Wai'oca's spirit flew from this world.

After four days, Wa-tyuonyi walked back to the spring and entered the place of the Pa'waa. He found Wai'oca and Mo-kaite living there together. Since that time, those three have lived in that place, for there was plenty of food, shelter, and stories to keep them until the spirits decide otherwise.

THE BEAR WOMAN
Dine (Navajo)

Near the Chuska Mountains, in the time of the ancient ancestors, there lived a beautiful young woman. She was the sister of twelve brothers, all of whom had divine powers. Because of her beauty and her family, this young woman was much sought after by warriors, hunters, and other great leaders who wanted to marry her. But she was very proud and refused them all. This caused her to be noticed by the Sun God and others of the Holy People. She refused them as well, by making impossible demands that no one could meet.

It was in this way that she attracted the attention of Coyote. Now Coyote was a divine being himself, but he did not use his great powers for good. Instead, he caused great mischief for the people.

When Coyote heard of this proud, beautiful woman, he went at once to visit her. He found her alone in her hogan—all of her brothers were away. After greeting her, Coyote asked, "Why have you refused so many powerful beings who want to marry you?"

"I don't know why you bother to ask," replied the young woman, "since you could never hope to accomplish even one of the things I require."

Three times Coyote asked and three times the woman made the same answer; but when Coyote asked the fourth time, she said, "Well, to begin with, I would not even think of marrying anyone until he has killed one of the Naye'i." The Naye'i were great monsters who roamed the world at that time, preying on the people.

When Coyote heard this, he left the woman and journeyed to the home of Yelapahi, Brown Giant, who was, of course, one of the Naye'i. He found Yelapahi putting the finishing touches on a sweathouse he was building.

Coyote helped Yelapahi finish the lodge and suggested that they sweat together. Once they were inside the darkened sweathouse, Coyote began to talk about what a slow runner Brown Giant was. This was true, for Brown Giant was as slow as cooling lava when he tried to run. "Your enemies make fun of you because of this," said Coyote. "But I can teach you a ceremony here in the sweathouse that will help you. You must break your own legs and spit on them. They will heal stronger and faster than ever. I have often done this myself, and you know how fast I am."

Now Brown Giant knew that Coyote was a swift runner. So, howling with pain, he pounded his legs with a rock until the bones shattered. He spit on them and began singing as Coyote had instructed. But his bones did not grow together. While he lay on the floor of the sweathouse helpless, Coyote killed him with his own weapons. Then he took Brown Giant's quiver and arrows to show to the young woman.

When Coyote reached her hogan, he said, "Here are the weapons of a Naye'i I have killed. Now you must marry me."

"No," said the woman, "I have not told you all that you must do. You must also be able to die four times and, each time, come back to life."

"That is all I must do?" asked Coyote.

"I speak the truth," answered the girl.

"Then let us play this game," Coyote said.

The young woman took Coyote outside, made him lie on the ground, and pounded him with a great club. But she did not crush the very point of his nose or the tip of his tail, which was where Coyote kept his life force.

The young woman returned to her hogan and went about her work. In a few minutes, there was Coyote in the doorway, saying, "I have won one game. Let's play another."

Twice more, the young woman beat Coyote with the club and left him for dead. Each time it took Coyote a little longer to pull himself back together, but each time he appeared in her doorway, saying, "I have won another game."

The fourth time she beat Coyote into pieces and scattered them in the air; she still failed to crush his nose and the tip of his tail. That time, it took Coyote so long to return to life that the girl was sure she was rid of him. Finally he entered her door again.

The young woman had no choice then to but marry him as she had sworn on her honor and that of her family. And so the beautiful, proud young woman became the wife of Coyote. But this was not as bad as the young woman had feared. Coyote was so proud of winning his beautiful young wife that he was very kind and gentle with her.

As the days passed, the young woman realized that she had come to care very deeply for her husband. Coyote had even begun to teach her some of the magic that he knew. Perhaps they would have gone on that way if it had not been for the return of the young woman's brothers.

But when she heard them outside the hogan, she cried to Coyote, "You must hide. My brothers will not be happy that I have married you. They may even try to harm you." So Coyote hid behind a pile of skins and tried to be very quiet.

The brothers came in and greeted their sister, handing her a great piece of venison to cook. As she was building up the fire, one brother spoke, saying, "It smells as though an animal has been here! What is that stink?"

Three times the brother asked and the sister did not answer. But when he asked the fourth time, Coyote sprang out from his hiding place, crying, "It is I, your new brother-in-law."

As the young woman had feared, the brothers were very angry, and they demanded that Coyote leave the hogan. Forced to choose between her brothers and her new husband, the young woman left with Coyote, taking all her belongings with her. A short distance away, they stopped and Coyote built a brush arbor for shelter.

Now the youngest brother had followed the couple, determined to learn more about Coyote. As he watched in amazement, Coyote killed his wife four times, and four times she restored herself to life. The youngest brother returned at once to the hogan and told the others what he had seen. "This is evil," said the oldest brother. "He is teaching her his magic. Soon she will be like him."

The next morning, as the brothers were leaving on a hunt, Coyote asked to come with them. Three times the brothers refused. But when Coyote asked the fourth time, they agreed to take him along. They traveled together into the mountains until they came to the Forbidden Canyon. The canyon was home to many dangerous and evil creatures but was forbidden to all others. So the brothers drew a rainbow across the sky to make a bridge and cross over the canyon.

Finally they came to a mesa where they could see the tracks of four bighorn sheep. The brothers sent Coyote to chase them out of the brush. Working together, they killed the sheep.

The brothers wrapped the meat into a great bundle. Then, using their powers, they shrank it into a pack small enough for Coyote to carry. "Take this back to the hogan," said the oldest brother. "We will continue the hunt. Since we are not with you to build the bridge, you must go around the canyon, not through it. Remember what we say—and do not open the bundle of meat until you reach home."

Coyote promised he would do as he was told. But as soon as he was out of the brothers' sight, he cut open the bundle, meaning to cook a small piece of meat to eat. At once the meat swelled to its normal size, and because it was too much to carry, Coyote had to leave most of it on the ground. And, of course, being Coyote, he walked straight into the Forbidden Canyon.

Later, as the brothers returned home, they passed the place where Coyote had left the meat. Just as they suspected, Coyote had not listened to the things they had said. Satisfied that they were rid of Coyote forever, they returned to their hogan. But that night, when there was no sign of her husband, the young woman became convinced that her brothers had tricked him. In a rage, she began to work the magic Coyote had taught her.

First, she walked in a circle around the fire. Next, she broke a tooth from her mouth and pushed in its place the sharp point of a sewing awl. She did this twice, and the points grew into long, pointed tusks. Hair began to grow all over her until she was covered with a thick coat of shaggy fur. Her face began to change and her nails turned into claws.

In the morning, when the brothers emerged from the hogan, the air was shattered by a bellowing roar. A great female bear rushed past them, following the trail Coyote had taken. That night the bear returned, covered with wounds. She had gone to the Forbidden Canyon to slay the monsters she thought had killed her husband. All night the brothers listened to her roars, as she worked the magic to heal herself. For three more days, Bear Woman sought revenge for the loss of Coyote. She slew most of the evil beings in the Forbidden Canyon, and the rest fled before her wrath. At night she worked magic to heal her wounds.

During this time, her brothers hid in their hogan. But on the fifth day, they were forced to hunt. They divided into small hunting parties, three going east, three south, three west and two to the north. The youngest brother was left at home to guard the hogan from Bear Woman's anger.

When the others had gone, the youngest brother used his powers to summon the help of Whirlwind. Whirlwind showed him how to dig a hole in the center of the hogan in which to hide. He gave him weapons to use, among them an arrow made of lightning and a stone knife as big as a hand. He set Wind at the boy's right ear to guard him by day and Darkness at his left ear to watch by night.

When Bear Woman awoke, she ran to the hogan and found her brothers had left. Angrily, she poured water on the ground to find the direction her brothers had taken. The water pooled and flowed east. Bear Woman ran in that direction, tracked her brothers, and killed three of them.

Bear Woman returned to the hogan and poured more water. This water flowed south. So she set off in that direction, found three more of her brothers, and killed them, too. When the water sent her west, she tracked and killed three more. At last she headed north and killed her two oldest brothers.

Now Bear Woman went back to the hogan to find her youngest brother. But when she poured the water this time, it sank into the earth. She began to sniff and scratch the dirt floor of the hogan. In its center, where the dirt was still soft, she dug her way into the hole that hid her youngest brother. "Come out and talk with me, little brother," Bear Woman said in a soft voice. Then she reached one great claw into the hole to pull out her brother.

At that moment, Wind whispered into the boy's ear, saying, "Climb out for yourself, or she will throw you at her feet and kill you."

Quickly the boy climbed out of the hole and rushed from the hogan. Bear Woman charged at him, but the boy spoke to her, saying, "Remember me. I am your brother."

Bear Woman stopped, her anger mingled with her old love for him. "Come inside the hogan," she said, "and we will talk."

But as they approached the hogan, Wind whispered, "Let us not enter. There is sorrow inside." So the boy would not enter. And since that time, the Dine will not enter a hogan where death or some great trouble has happened.

"If you will not come inside, then sit facing the West," Bear Woman said, "and I will comb your hair."

"Do not listen," Wind said. "Face north so you can watch her shadow." So the boy sat facing north, and Bear Woman loosed his long hair and began to comb it. By watching her shadow, the boy could see when her great jaws stretched out toward his neck. Four times this happened; and four times the boy spoke to her and she drew back.

Then Wind whispered to the youngest brother, "The next time she reaches for you, she will kill you. In that bush over there, where the squirrel sits chattering, she has hidden her heart. Destroy it and you destroy her."

When Bear Woman again stretched her jaws toward him, the boy jumped up and ran toward the bush. Snarling, Bear Woman charged after him, but cactus and yuccas grew in her path and slowed her chase. The youngest brother reached the bush and flung his lightning arrow into Bear Woman's heart. Blood poured from it and Bear Woman fell with blood flowing from her side. The stream of blood from her heart and the stream of blood from her body spread toward each other over the sand.

"Do not let the streams of blood reach each other," Wind cried, "or she will live again, more powerful than before." So the youngest brother took the stone knife and drew a great gash in the dirt between the two streams. The blood ceased its flow, and Bear Woman was still.

The youngest brother took the head of Bear Woman and placed it on the ground under a piñion tree. "You will live again in this bear form," he said, "but not as a creature of evil. Although you may fight to defend yourself, you will live in service to the people and you will not quarrel with them." When the boy finished speaking, the head rose and a bear's body grew from the earth. The bear looked at the boy and then turned and walked away into the mountains.

All of this happened a long time ago, and bears have lived as friends of the Dine ever since. As for Coyote and his adventures in the Forbidden Canyon, that is another story.

THE BEAUTY WAY—
THE CEREMONY OF
WHITE-PAINTED WOMAN
Apache

*Long ago, the world was filled with evil giants and
monsters who preyed on the Apache people. At that time,
White-Painted Woman married the Sun. She gave birth to
a boy—Child of Water—who slew the enemies of the
people. White-Painted Woman watched as her son made
the world safe for the Apache. Then she gave birth to a
daughter. And when she saw that First Girl Child was
becoming a woman, White-Painted Woman gave the
people the Beauty Way ceremony. She taught First Girl
Child to do this dance, to follow the ceremony. In this
way, First Girl Child became as White-Painted Woman,
and the people could continue.*

Dahazi stood very still and listened to the words of the
old medicine man as he told the story of White-Painted
Woman, the mythical spirit being of the Apache people.
The first rays of sun had turned the tops of the
mountains to gold. But here on the valley floor, the light
was still gray and the early morning mist swirled around
her. Dahazi was too excited and too nervous to be cold,
though. Her entrance into womanhood—her Beauty Way
Ceremony—had begun.

Dahazi knew that her family had begun preparing for
this ceremony when she was only a little girl. In the past

few months, the preparations had reached a fever pitch. Everything must be exactly right: Dahazi's dress, the regalia of the dancers, the prayers and songs, and the steps of the dance. To spoil this ceremony could bring disaster to the people.

Dahazi wore an ankle-length skirt of bright yellow; the color symbolizing pollen, the bringer of life. Over the long-tiered skirt, she wore a beautiful deerskin shirt trimmed with fringes, which swayed from the bottom of her blouse and from her long sleeves. Jingle bells danced from the hem of her skirt and from the fringes of the blouse, which was decorated with a bright-rayed sun, a full moon, and a rainbow. A beaded necklace with intricate designs hung to Dahazi's waist, and a matching headband encircled her forehead. An eagle feather was tied in her long, shiny black hair.

Standing next to Dahazi was her god-spirit mother. This elder woman would guide and teach Dahazi throughout the four-day ceremony. Dahazi was grateful that the woman her parents had chosen was a close friend. Her presence was warm and comforting. Like Dahazi, Spirit Mother wore knee-high buckskin moccasins adorned with jingle bells.

As the sun rose, it was time to build the sacred lodge that would be Dahazi's home for the four days of the ceremony. Once the lodge was completed, the old medicine man whom her parents had selected to conduct the ceremony brought out a great basket of pollen and blessed it. Then he blessed Dahazi and marked her forehead, cheeks, nose, and chin with the yellow pollen.

Now the medicine man handed the basket to Dahazi, and the people lined up in front of her. She marked the face of anyone who was sad or sick or in need of special healing. When she was finished, a blanket was spread on the ground next to the sacred lodge. Dahazi was lowered to the blanket and Spirit Mother knelt beside her. Gently Spirit Mother began to run her hands over Dahazi's arms and legs, feeling the "spirit strength" or purity of the young woman's body. As her hands worked, she prayed in low, soft tones. Then Dahazi was lifted to her feet.

White-Painted Woman had taught the people that a girl's body must open to accept the spirits that will enable her to create new life. Yet she must be strong in heart and spirit to refuse evil influences that are attracted to her openness.

The Drumming Society gathered next to the sacred lodge, each member carrying a small hand drum and a drumstick with a long curved handle. As they began to play and sing, a basket was brought out and filled with fruit, candy, and small bundles of pollen. The medicine man carried this basket some distance from the lodge and set it on the ground. At his sign, Dahazi ran to the basket, circled it, and returned to the lodge. Four times this was done, with the basket being moved closer to the lodge for each run. Then Dahazi and Spirit Mother turned to enter the sacred lodge. Behind her, Dahazi could hear the crowd's shouts and laughter as the fruit and candy were thrown to them. These tokens of the ritual brought good luck and fortune to the people.

Pitched just behind the sacred lodge was her family's

tepee, and Dahazi could hear her mother's voice, snapping out orders as her sisters and her cousins laid out the food for this, the first feast served. For the next four days, her family would host these feasts, feeding everyone who had gathered here. When the food was ready, Dahazi was brought from the lodge to bless it before going back inside with Spirit Mother.

All day Dahazi listened carefully as Spirit Mother talked of the changes that were happening to her. Spirit Mother spoke of men and what it would be like to be married and have children. Then she spoke of White-Painted Woman:

White-Painted Woman watched and guided her son, Child of Water, as he slew the enemies of the people. Though she feared for him, she did not try to stop him as he sought danger and faced death again and again. In this way, she showed the Apache that children do not belong to their parents but to all the people.

Dahazi listened, for she knew these ancient teachings were important to her new life as a woman.

When the sun had set, the men began building the great pyre of wood that would burn through all four nights of the ceremony. At full dark, Dahazi and Spirit Mother came out to stand beside the sacred lodge. It was time for one of the most beautiful and powerful parts of the Beauty Way—the Crown Dancers!

When White-Painted Woman taught the Beauty Way to the people, she knew First Girl Child must be guarded and protected. She called on the mountain spirits to shield the people. These were the Crown Dancers.

Dahazi's heartbeat quickened to the sound of the

drum as the Crown Dancers stepped from the darkness into the firelight. In quick, jerky steps, the Crown Dancers circled the fire. The light threw long, grotesque shadows of the dancers on the ground as they thrust their arms, legs, and heads into the movements of the dance. The sounds of the bells on their ankles mingled with the piercing shrieks of the dancers.

Cavorting among the Crown Dancers was the little Clown Dancer, dressed all in one color. It was his job to deflect all evil from the dance ground. Between songs, he scurried around, clearing debris that might cause a dancer a misstep. Dahazi smiled as she watched. Although she could not "officially" know this, the distinctive skip and the ringing laugh of her six-year-old nephew were unmistakable.

The Crown Dancers finished their first round of dances and retreated into the darkness. Dahazi's heart beat quicker; it was her turn! She followed Spirit Mother into the lodge. The old medicine man sat down outside the lodge. Dahazi heard the beat of his drum; she heard him begin the song. Inside the lodge, standing before Spirit Mother, Dahazi began to sway to the movements of the dance, the dance given to First Girl Child by White-Painted Woman, a dance as old as the Apache people and as young as Dahazi herself.

All night long, the dances continued; alternating between the Crown Dancers and Dahazi in her sacred lodge. The people formed a circle at the edge of the area and danced around the Crown Dancers. Families and friends visited, and children raced through the crowd, playing games and laughing. As the sun rose, Dahazi returned to the sacred lodge. She would spend the day resting, learning from Spirit Mother, and coming out to bless the food for the feasts hosted by her family. At night the dancing would begin again.

As the sun rose after the fourth night of dancing, the people formed two great lines in front of the sacred lodge. The medicine man again brought the great basket filled with fruit and candy. He carried it between the rows of people and set it on the ground. Carefully he placed an eagle feather in the basket and signaled Dahazi to begin her run. Four times she ran, and this time each run was longer, as the medicine man moved the basket farther and farther away. The fourth time Dahazi circled the basket, she reached down and plucked the feather from the fruit and candy, carrying it with her. This feather symbolized the entrance of White-Painted Woman into her new life. It was a sacred gift from the medicine man who conducted the ceremony.

As Dahazi plucked the feather and ran from the dance ground, the men gave a great shout and pulled the poles of the sacred lodge apart. The people lined up to be blessed by the medicine man and to have their faces marked with red ocher and cornmeal paste. It was time for the last feast and the great giveaway of specially chosen gifts to honor the medicine man, Spirit Mother, the dancers, and everyone else who had participated in the ceremony. As Dahazi sat with her family, she felt a warm glow deep inside. On this day, she was First Girl Child no longer. On this day, she had become White-Painted Woman.

THE NORTHWEST

Few areas of North America vary as much in climate and geography as the Northwest. It includes the northern plains, where a way of life developed around the horse and the hunting of buffalo. Here women were often as good at riding as the men. In the plateau and Pacific coast regions of Washington, Oregon, and northern California, the abundance of natural plant foods gathered by the women made them centrally important as providers. At the far north, where Native people adapted to Arctic conditions, the clothing designed and sewn by women made survival possible. Although the women lived in cultures that differed greatly, their importance to the life of the people was one thing all these Native tribal nations have always shared.

One of the lessons taught by stories dealing with the rites of passage of girls is the necessity of showing respect for tradition. Among the Luiseño and many other Native peoples of California, a special ceremony was performed for a girl entering womanhood. At its center is a sand painting, made to symbolize the world and the forces of creation that a girl joins when she becomes a woman. The story "How Pelican Girl Was Saved" takes place after such ceremony. It shows what happens when a young woman does not take care to follow the rules set forth to

govern her behavior after she has completed that powerful rite of passage. As a result of her carelessness, a dangerous being from the land of the spirits, which is described by the Miwok people as the North World, is drawn to Pelican Girl, and abducts her. Only through the intervention of Coyote, who helps the people when they are in trouble, can Pelican Girl be restored to her family and things made right again.

"Where the Girl Rescued Her Brother" has always been one of my favorite tales from the 1870s. At that time, the Cheyenne, one of the buffalo-hunting nations of the Plains, were engaged in a struggle to maintain their traditional lands and lifestyle against overwhelming odds. They did so in many cases not only with courage but an incredible sense of honor. Women and men alike were expected to show courage and coolness in the face of danger. I can think of no story that better exemplifies those qualities than this tale about the battle near Rosebud Creek in present-day Montana, a fight that took place only a few days before the Lakota and Cheyenne victory against the forces of Lieutenant Colonel George Armstrong Custer at Little Bighorn.

In telling "Chipmunk Girl and Owl Woman," which follows the familiar Native device of using the animal people to convey a tale about human beings, I have patterned my version after a telling by Mourning Dove, the Okanagan writer and storyteller. The story conveys important lessons, including both the idea of not trusting strangers and the role elders play in protecting the young.

If a young girl is to go out on her own, she must know who to trust and how to avoid dangerous situations. She must also have the freedom to learn—sometimes by making her own mistakes—how to make the right decisions when no older person is around to tell her what to do. Chipmunk Girl's lessons are learned the hard way and are thus much more memorable as a rite of passage.

"The Girl Who Married the Moon" comes from a Native tradition in which the sun is viewed as a woman and the moon as a man. The Alutiiq people of Kodiak Island, like many peoples of the northwestern coast, had a great reputation as mask makers. When Moon goes to carry on his duties in the night sky, it is one of his masks that is seen by the people on earth. The young woman who marries him is like Pandora of classical Greek mythology—she cannot control her curiosity. Instead of suffering for what she discloses, however, she ends up a more equal partner with her husband because she shows that she has the strength and ability to help him with his work. It is yet another example of the Native American affirmation of the capability of women.

HOW PELICAN GIRL WAS SAVED
Lake Miwok

Long ago, in the land of the South People, the time had come for Pelican Girl's dance. It was the special one always given for girls about to become women. All the people of Middle Village gathered for her dance. Coyote, the great warrior, was there with his wife, Frog Woman. Coyote's grandson, Hawk Chief, was there. Hawk Chief had agreed to be Pelican Girl's husband when she became a woman. Small Hawk and Blue Jay, Robin and Crested Bird were there, too. Little Owl, who was a great doctor, Hummingbird, and the two Snipe Girls also were there. Everyone went into the sweathouse and danced on the great wooden drum for four days. All the right ceremonies were done for Pelican Girl.

When the dance was finished, the women of Middle Village took Pelican Girl to the women's house. There she stayed until the moon had grown small in the sky and then returned to its full size again. At last the women took Pelican Girl out of the house. They put beads around her neck. They put beads around her wrists and ankles.

"Stay close to the village," they told her.

But as Pelican Girl sat there, the Snipe Girls came walking by.

"Where are you going?" Pelican Girl called to them.

"We are going to pick clover," they said.

"I want to come with you," Pelican Girl said.

"You can come with us," the Snipe Girls said. "Bring along your pack basket. We'll pick the clover for you. Then it will be all right."

Pelican Girl and her friends went to her mother. "The Snipe Girls are going out to gather clover. I want to go with them. I am going with them," she said.

"No," her mother said. "That is not right. It's too soon after your dance. Women never go around so soon after that! You have to stay close to home."

When her mother said that, Pelican Girl started to cry.

"I am going to go. I am going to go," she said as she cried.

Finally her mother gave in. "You can go with the Snipe Girls," she said. "But you must be careful. Remember, you are not supposed to pick up anything. Let them pick the clover for you and put it into your basket."

"We shall do that," the Snipe Girls said. Then Pelican Girl took her basket, and the three of them walked out of the village.

They walked and walked, heading toward the north until they reached the meadow. It was full of clover, and the Snipe Girls began to pick it. They put it into their baskets and Pelican Girl's basket. Pelican Girl was careful to do as she had been told. She did not pick up anything but just walked along, carrying the basket on her back.

It was late in the afternoon when their baskets were filled and they started back toward the village. Pelican

Girl walked along slowly, looking at things while her two friends walked on ahead. Soon they came to a turn in the trail and disappeared behind a small hill. But Pelican Girl did not notice that her friends were out of sight. There, right in the middle of the trail, was a big goose. It appeared to have fallen from the sky.

"Look at this!" Pelican Girl said. "My uncles can use its feathers. We should pick up this goose and take it home."

When no one answered her, Pelican Girl realized that her friends were too far ahead to hear her voice. So, without even thinking, she bent down, picked up the goose, and put it into her pack basket. She started walking toward the turn where her friends had disappeared. As she walked, her pack basket seemed to grow heavier and heavier with each step. At the turn, it became so heavy she could hardly walk. Then she began to hear a voice.

"*Hoshh, hoshh, hoshh, hoshh,*" the voice sang out. It came from inside the pack basket on her back.

Pelican Girl could walk no farther. Her pack was so heavy that she had to sit down. She took it from her back, and the singing continued.

"*Hoshh, hoshh, hoshh, hoshh.*"

Pelican Girl tried to stand up, but she could not move. A strange person stood in front of her basket.

"Grandchild," he sang out, in a voice that seemed to come from the spirit world, "I want those beads around your neck."

Pelican Girl knew who he was. He was the Shoko, a powerful person from the North World, where the fire-eaters live. He had disguised himself as a goose so that she would pick him up. By doing this, Pelican Girl had given him the power to carry her away to his land. Now the Shoko began to dance around her as he sang.

"*Hoshh, hoshh, hoshh, hoshh.*"

Pelican Girl reached up with a trembling hand and pulled the beads from her neck. She threw them at the Shoko, who caught them in one hand and started to dance away. But before he had gone far, he turned.

"Grandchild," he sang out, "*hoshh, hoshh, hoshh, hoshh.* I want those beads around your wrists. That is why I came back."

Pelican Girl pulled the beads from her wrists and threw them to the Shoko. Just as before, he danced away and then danced back again.

"Grandchild," he sang out, "*hoshh, hoshh, hoshh, hoshh.* I want those beads around your ankles. That is why I came back."

Pelican Girl pulled the beads from her ankles, but again the Shoko danced a little way and returned.

"Grandchild," he sang out, "*hoshh, hoshh, hoshh, hoshh.* I want one more thing. That is why I came back."

Then Shoko grabbed Pelican Girl, put her under one arm, and danced off with her. He carried her with him to the North World, where he hid her in the pit under the drum in his dance house.

In the meantime, the Snipe Girls had returned to Middle Village.

"Where is Pelican Girl?" people asked them. "She went with you to pick clover. Didn't she come back with you?"

The Snipe Girls were frightened. "We don't know where she is," they said. "As we went around the hill at the edge of the village, she was right behind us. We heard her say, 'Look at this! My uncles can use its feathers.' But when we turned back for her, we saw her pack basket in the middle of the trail and she was gone."

"We must go look for my grandson's wife-to-be," Coyote, the wise one, said. "Blue Jay, you are the best tracker. You can lead us on the search."

So they all went to look for Pelican Girl. Blue Jay led them to the place in the trail where she had disappeared.

"Someone has carried her away," Blue Jay said. "That is what these tracks tell me."

"My daughter is dead," said Pelican Girl's mother, and she began to cry.

But Coyote was looking around. He studied very carefully the tracks that had been left behind, and he understood what had happened.

"Pelican Girl is not dead," he said. "The people of the North World, the fire-eaters, have taken her."

All of them took the trail to the North World, following Coyote. When they reached the top of the mountain, Coyote told everyone to stop.

"I can see the edge of the North World," Coyote said. "There are fighting men along it, ready with their bows and arrows. Because Pelican Girl was going to marry my grandson, they know I will be coming to rescue her. We will not be able to get across this way. We must make a plan."

Then the people talked about what could be done. It was decided that they would send Little Owl ahead. He would be able to use his power to help them. So Little

Owl took the shape of a bird of the night. He flew over the line of fighting men and they did not see him. He whispered into their ears.

"Coyote is not coming now," he whispered. "Go to sleep and rest so that you'll be ready to fight him tomorrow."

The fighting men listened to Little Owl's words. They had been on watch ever since Shoko had brought Pelican Girl to the North World. They were tired. One by one, they fell asleep with their bows and arrows in their hands.

Coyote was watching from the mountaintop. As soon as all the fighting men were asleep, he turned to the people with him.

"I am going to put you into my sack," Coyote said. Then he turned the South People into mice and put them into the sack hung around his neck. Carrying the South People with him, Coyote sneaked across the line into the North World.

When they got to the dance house, they found Shoko and all the North People asleep. Coyote let the mouse people out of his sack. They went around tying together the long hair of the sleeping people, chewing through their bowstrings and chewing through the sinew wrapping that held the stone heads on their spears and arrows.

After their work was done, they changed back into people and began to look for Pelican Girl. They stepped over the sleeping bodies of the North People as they searched. Finally they found her, hidden under the big wooden dance drum. She was very sick and could not move. So the people carried her. But as they were leaving the dance house, Small Hawk tripped over the legs of one of the North People and woke him.

"Wake up!" the man shouted. "Wake up! There are strangers in our dance house!"

The North People tried to stand, but they fell back because their long hair had been tied together. As the North People stumbled, Coyote and all the others ran out taking Pelican Girl with them. By the time the North People had untied their long hair, Coyote and his friends were halfway home.

Now the North People grabbed their bows and arrows and their spears. But their weapons fell apart because the mice had chewed through the sinew. By the time the North People fixed their weapons, Coyote and the others had crossed the line into the South World. They escaped, carrying Pelican Girl back to Middle Village.

Pelican Girl was sick for a long time. The North People had turned her into a fire-eater. Little Owl had to work hard to cure her. He sang and danced all night for many nights. He made her stay in the sweathouse for many days to cleanse her body and spirit. At last she was well again. She and Hawk Chief were married, and everyone in Middle Village came to their wedding.

Because of her experience and all that she learned, Pelican Girl became one of the women who taught the young girls how to behave when the time came for their initiations into womanhood. Thanks to Pelican Girl, none of the young girls ever made the mistakes she had made.

That is the story of how Pelican Girl was saved and became a wise woman among her people.

WHERE THE GIRL RESCUED HER BROTHER
Cheyenne

It was the moon when the chokecherries were ripe. A young woman rode out of a Cheyenne camp with her husband and her brother. The young woman's name was Buffalo Calf Road Woman. Her husband, Black Coyote, was one of the chiefs of the Cheyenne, the people of the plains who call themselves Tsis-tsis-tas, meaning simply "The People." Buffalo Calf Road Woman's brother, Comes-in-Sight, was also one of the Cheyenne chiefs, and it was well-known how close he was to his sister.

Like many of the other young women of the Cheyenne, Buffalo Calf Road Woman was respected for her honorable nature. Although it was the men who most often went to war to defend the people — as they were doing on this day—women would accompany their husbands when they went to battle. If a man held an important position among the Cheyenne, such as the keeper of the Sacred Arrows, then his wife, too, would have to be of the highest moral character, for she shared the weight of his responsibility.

Buffalo Calf Road Woman was well aware of this, and as she rode by her husband she did so with pride. She knew that today they were on their way to meet their old allies, the Lakota. They were going out to try to drive back the *veho*, the spider people who were trying to claim all the lands of the Native peoples.

The Cheyenne had been worried about the *vého*, the white people, for a long time. They had given them that name because, like the black widow spider, they were very beautiful but it was dangerous to get close to them. And unlike the Cheyenne, they seemed to follow a practice of making promises and not keeping them. Although their soldier chief Custer had promised to be friendly with the Cheyenne, now he and the others had come into their lands to make war upon them.

Buffalo Calf Road Woman wore a robe embroidered with porcupine quills. The clothing of her brother and her husband, Black Coyote, was also beautifully decorated with those quills, which had been flattened, dyed in different colors, folded, and sewed on in patterns. Buffalo Calf Road Woman was proud that she belonged to the Society of Quilters. As with the men's societies, only a few women—those of the best character—could join. Like the men, the women had to be strong, honorable, and brave. Buffalo Calf Road Woman had grown up hearing stories of how Cheyenne women would defend their families when the men were away. The women of the Cheyenne were brave, and those in the Society of Quilters were the bravest of all.

Buffalo Calf Road Woman smiled as she remembered one day when the women of the Society of Quilters showed such bravery. It was during the Moon of Falling Leaves. A big hunt had been planned. The men who acted as scouts had gone out and located the great buffalo herd. They had seen, too, that there were no human enemies anywhere near their camp. So almost none of the men remained behind.

On that day, when all the men were away, a great grizzly bear came into the camp. Such things seldom happened, but this bear was one that had been wounded in the leg by a white fur-trapper's bullet. It could no longer hunt as it had before, and hunger brought it to the Cheyenne camp, where it smelled food cooking.

When the huge bear came walking into the camp, almost everyone scattered. Some women grabbed their little children. Old people shut the door flaps of their tepees, and the boys ran to find their bows and arrows. Only a group of seven women who had been working on the embroidery of an elk-skin robe did not run. They were members of the Society of Quilters, and Buffalo Calf Road Woman was among them. The seven women put down their work, picked up the weapons they had close to hand, and stood to face the grizzly bear.

Now of all of the animals of the plains, the only one fierce enough and powerful enough to attack a human was the grizzly. But confronted by that determined group of women, the grizzly bear stopped in its tracks. It had come to steal food, not fight. The head of the Society of Quilters stepped forward a pace and spoke to the bear.

"Grandfather," she said, her voice low and firm, "we do not wish to harm you, but we will protect our camp. Go back to your own home."

The grizzly shook its head and then turned and walked out of the camp. The women stood and watched it as it went down through the cottonwoods and was lost from sight along the bend of the stream.

Buffalo Calf Road Woman turned her mind away from her memories. They were close to Rosebud Creek. The scouts had told them that a great number of the *veho* soldiers would be there and that the Gray Fox, General George Crook, was in command. The Cheyenne had joined up now with the Oglala, led by Crazy Horse. The Lakota people were always friends to the Cheyenne, but this man, Crazy Horse, was the best friend of all. Some even said that he was one of their chiefs, too, as well as being a war leader of his Oglala.

There were Crow and Shoshone scouts with Crook, and the *veho* had many cannons. The Lakota and the Cheyenne were outnumbered by the two thousand men in Crook's command. But they were prepared to fight. They had put on their finest clothes, for no man should risk his life without being dressed well enough so that if he died, the enemy would know a great warrior had fallen. Some of the men raised their headdresses three times, calling out their names and the deeds they had done. Those headdresses of eagle feathers were thought to give magical protection to a warrior. Other men busied themselves painting designs on their war ponies.

Now they could hear Crook's army approaching. The rumble of the horses' hooves echoed down the valley, and there was the sound of trumpets. War ponies reared up and stomped their feet. Many of the Cheyenne men found it hard to put on the last of their paint as their hands shook from the excitement of the coming battle.

Crazy Horse vaulted onto his horse and held up one arm. "*Hoka Hey,*" he cried. "It is a good day to die."

Buffalo Calf Road Woman watched from a hill as the

two lines of men—the blue soldiers to one side, and the Lakota and Cheyenne to the other—raced toward each other. The battle began. It was not a quick fight or an easy one. There were brave men on both sides. Two Moons, Little Hawk, Yellow Eagle, Sitting Bull, and Crazy Horse were only a few of the great warriors who fought for the Cheyenne and the Lakota. And Crook, the Gray Fox general of the whites, was known to be a tough fighter and a worthy enemy.

Buffalo Calf Road Woman's husband, Black Coyote, and her brother, Comes-in-Sight, were in the thick of the fight. The odds in the battle were almost even. Although the whites had more soldiers and guns, the Lakota and the Cheyenne were better shots and better horsemen. Had it not been for the Crow and Shoshone scouts helping Crook, the white soldiers might have broken quickly from the ferocity of the attack.

From one side to the other, groups of men attacked and retreated as the guns cracked, cannons boomed, and smoke filled the air. The war shouts of the Lakota and the Cheyenne were almost as loud as the rumble of the guns. The sun moved across the sky as the fight went on, hour after hour, while the confusion of battle swirled below.

Then Buffalo Calf Road Woman saw something that horrified her. Her brother had been drawn off to one side, surrounded by Crow scouts. He tried to ride free of them, but his pony went down, struck by a rifle bullet and killed. Now he was on foot, still fighting. The Crow warriors were trying to get close, to count coup on him. It was more of an honor to touch a living enemy, so they were not firing their rifles at him. And he was able to keep them away with his bow and arrows. But it was clear that soon he would be out of ammunition and would fall to the enemy.

Buffalo Calf Road Woman waited no longer. She dug her heels into her pony's sides and galloped down the hill. Her head low, her braids streaming behind her, she rode into the heart of the fight. Some men moved aside as they saw her coming, for there was a determined look in her eyes. She made the long howling cry that Cheyenne women used to urge on the warriors. This time, however, she was the one going into the fight. Her voice was as strong as an eagle's. Her horse scattered the ponies of the Crow scouts who were closing in on her brother, Comes-in-Sight. She held out a hand; her brother grabbed it and vaulted onto the pony behind her. Then she wheeled, ducking the arrows of the Crow scouts, and heading back up the hill.

That was when it happened. For a moment, it seemed as if all the shooting stopped. The Cheyenne and the Lakota, and even the *veho* soldiers, lowered their guns to watch this act of great bravery. A shout went up, not from one side but from both, as Buffalo Calf Road Woman reached the safety of the hilltop again, her brother safe behind her on her horse. White men and Indians cheered her.

So it was that Buffalo Calf Road Woman performed the act for which the people would always remember her. Inspired by her courage, the Cheyenne and Lakota drove back the Gray Fox—Crook made a strategic withdrawal.

"Even the *veho* general was impressed," said the

Cheyenne people. "He saw that if our women were that brave, he would stand no chance against us in battle."

So it is that to this day, the Cheyenne and the Lakota people do not refer to the fight as the Battle of the Rosebud. Instead, they honor Buffalo Calf Road Woman by calling the fight Where the Girl Rescued Her Brother.

CHIPMUNK GIRL AND OWL WOMAN

Okanagan

Chipmunk Girl lived with her grandmother in the woods. She liked nothing better than to pick berries. She would walk through the woods happily picking berries, eating some, and putting the rest into the pouch that hung at her side.

Her favorite bush was the serviceberry. She would go to that bush every day, climb up into it, and gather those berries and eat them until she could hold no more. As she picked them, Chipmunk Girl would sing a little song:

> One berry ripe,
> Two berries ripe,
> Three berries ripe!

One day, as she sat in the bush eating berries, she heard footsteps below her. When she looked down, there was Owl Woman, looking back up at her with big hungry eyes. Owl Woman carried a large basket on her back. She went from village to village stealing children, and in that basket were the little children she had stolen. Whenever she became hungry, she would take out some of those children and eat them.

Chipmunk's grandmother had told her about Owl Woman. She had told Chipmunk to be careful of dangerous people like Owl Woman and not ever to talk to them. But Chipmunk was not afraid. She knew that she was high up in the bush. Owl Woman could never reach her there.

"Chipmunk Girl," Owl Woman said in a sweet voice, "your father is calllling yooou. He wants yooou to come hooome right now."

"My father died many winters ago," Chipmunk Girl answered.

Owl Woman was quiet as she thought about what to do. Then she spoke again.

"Chipmunk Girl," she said in an even sweeter voice, "your mother is calllling yooou."

"I have no mother," Chipmunk Girl said. "She died long ago."

Owl Woman was not certain what to do next. She stood there for a long long time thinking. Then she spoke once more.

"Chipmunk Girl, your aunt is calllling yooou. She wants yooou to come hooome right now."

Chipmunk Girl began to laugh. "I do not have an aunt," she said. "I never had an aunt."

"I did not mean toooo say that," Owl Woman said. "It is your uncle. Your uncle is calllling yooou. He wants yooou to come hooome right now."

Chipmunk Girl laughed even harder at that lie. "I do not have an uncle. I never had an uncle."

Owl Woman was not happy. She stood there thinking for a long time. At last she spoke again.

"Chipmunk Girl," she cooed, "your grandfather is calllling yooou. He wants yooou to come hooome right now."

Chipmunk Girl laughed even harder than before. "I do not have a grandfather," she said. "My grandfather died before I was born."

Owl Woman tried one last time.

"Chipmunk Girl," she said in her sweetest voice, "your grandmother is calllling yooou. She wants yooou to come hooome right now."

Then Chipmunk Girl did not know what to do. She wished she had never answered Owl Woman's first words. It was quite possible that her grandmother was calling her.

"Chipmunk Girl," Owl Woman said again, for she could see that her words were working this time. "Your grandmother is calllling yooou. She wants yooou to come hooome right now. Are you not going to come down from that bush?"

"I will not come down until you cover your eyes," Chipmunk Girl said.

"I will dooo sooo," Owl Woman said. She put her long skinny fingers over her face, but she held her fingers open just a little bit so that she could see through them.

Chipmunk Girl took a deep breath. Then, instead of climbing down from the bush, she jumped right over Owl Woman's head.

Owl Woman grabbed at her, but Chipmunk Girl had leaped too quickly. All that Owl Woman was able to do was to scratch the back of Chipmunk Girl's dress. And ever since then, all chipmunks have stripes down their backs from Owl Woman's claws.

Chipmunk Girl landed on the ground and ran as fast as she could, straight for her grandmother's tepee. The basketful of children on her back was heavy, and so Owl Woman was not as fast as Chipmunk Girl. But she still followed her trail.

When Chipmunk Girl reached her grandmother's tepee she rushed inside. She was so excited, she could barely speak. *"Sing-naw, sing-naw,"* she said to her grandmother. "Owl, owl."

"What is that?" said Chipmunk's grandmother, not hearing the word clearly. "Thorn? Thorn? Did you step on a thorn?"

"Owl," said Chipmunk Girl. "Owl Woman is after me. Help me hide."

Grandmother looked for a good place to hide Chipmunk Girl. But Owl Woman would surely look into that basket; she would know to look under that bed. Grandmother did not know what to do.

Then Meadowlark began to sing from outside.

> Hide her between
> those big oyster shells

That was a good place to hide. Grandmother put Chipmunk Girl between the oyster shells. And, remembering that Meadowlark loves to tell everyone else's secrets, she took off her white necklace.

"Take this and do not tell anyone where my granddaughter is hidden," Grandmother said, throwing the necklace to Meadowlark. It landed around his neck, and all meadowlarks wear that necklace to this day.

Soon Owl Woman reached Grandmother's house.

"I am hunting a child. Where is she hidden?" Owl Woman said. But Grandmother said nothing.

Owl Woman began to search for Chipmunk Girl. She looked in the basket. She looked under the bed. She even looked into the potful of soup. Chipmunk Girl was nowhere to be seen.

Then Meadowlark began to sing from the branch outside.

> I will tell you if you pay me
> I will tell you if you pay me
> I will tell you where she is

Owl Woman took off her yellow vest and threw it to Meadowlark, who caught it around his head. It hung down on his chest and looked very fine. So it is that meadowlarks all have a yellow vest now.

"Tellll me where the child I am hunting is hidden," Owl Woman said.

Then Meadowlark lifted up his head and sang;

> Between the oyster shells
> take her out
> Between the oyster shells
> take her out

Owl Woman looked between the oyster shells and found Chipmunk Girl. With her long sharp fingernails, she cut out Chipmunk Girl's heart and swallowed it.

"Eh, it is gooood," Owl Woman said. "The hearts of little girls are the best." And she walked away, carrying the basketful of children on her back.

Coyote, though, was watching from the bushes. He

spoke to Meadowlark. "See what you have done?" he said. "What can you do to make things right?" Then Coyote began to follow the trail of Owl Woman.

Grandmother wept and wept over the body of her granddaughter. But as she wept, she began to hear a voice singing. It was Meadowlark.

Use a berry for her heart
Use a berry for her heart

So Meadowlark kept singing.

Grandmother looked into Chipmunk Girl's little berry basket. There was just one serviceberry left in it. She put that berry into the place where Chipmunk Girl's heart had been and carefully sewed up the hole. Next she jumped over Chipmunk Girl's body, once, twice, three times. The third time, Chipmunk Girl sat up, brought back to life. From that day on, she always remembered everything Grandmother told her, and she took special care always to show respect to the berry bushes.

Meanwhile, Coyote caught up with Owl Woman.

"My friend," he said, "I see you have caught some little ones. I like to catch little ones, too, and eat them. Let me travel with you for a while. Together we will be able to catch even more of them."

Owl Woman was pleased. Coyote was known to be a good hunter. Together they would surely have good luck.

"Eh, that is gooood," Owl Woman said. "We will travel together."

They began to walk along. Before they had gone far,

Coyote spoke again. "I am hungry," he said. "Let us make a fire and cook those little ones you are carrying. We can always get more."

"Eh," Owl Woman said, "that is gooood." She put down the basket and began to gather sticks.

"No," Coyote said, "let these little ones work for us. They can gather the sticks."

Owl Woman liked that idea. She did as Coyote said. Then Coyote began to walk around, telling the little ones what to do in a harsh voice. When he was close to each child, though, he leaned over and whispered, "Gather wood with a lot of pitch. Be ready to do what I tell you."

Soon the fire was burning very hot. Owl Woman was ready to cook the little ones, but Coyote stopped her.

"You should paint your face and your body first," Coyote said. "This is an important feast. Use charcoal to paint yourself. We will put lots of pitch on your arms and legs and your face so the charcoal will stick to you."

Owl Woman liked that idea. Coyote and the little ones covered her legs and her arms and her face with pitch, and they put charcoal on her in beautiful patterns. She looked very fine.

"Eh," Owl Woman said, looking at herself, "it is goood. Let us eat nooow."

"No," Coyote said, "first we must dance—dance in a circle close to the fire."

Again Owl Woman did as Coyote said. She danced close to the fire. And as she danced, Coyote whispered to the little ones, "Listen carefully if you want to go home to your families. Get long forked sticks and be ready to do what I tell you," he said.

Coyote began to dance next to Owl Woman. That made her very happy. Every now and then he would give her a little push, and that made her laugh. Around and around they went. Owl Woman was growing tired, but Coyote would not let her stop.

"You are a fine dancer," he said. "I like to watch you dance."

So Owl Woman danced and danced. Coyote waited until she was very close to the fire. Then, with one big push, he shoved her so hard that she fell right into the flames. The pitch all over her body began to burn.

"Hold her in the fire," he called out to the children.

All of the little ones used their forked sticks to keep Owl Woman in the fire. Soon she burned up and nothing was left of her but ashes.

That is what happened long ago.

THE GIRL WHO MARRIED THE MOON
Alutiiq

Long ago, in the village of Chiniak, on the island of
Kodiak, there were two cousins. Like the other girls of
the village, they were skilled in many things. They knew
how to weave beautiful hats and baskets from spruce
roots. They were good at digging cranberry and other
roots and finding the berries that were ready to be
gathered in autumn. Like all the girls of their village, they
had always been shown much love and understanding
by their parents and the other elders. They had been
given the freedom to do whatever they wished, but they
had also been raised to be strong and brave. When they
were very small, they had been placed many times in the
cold salt water of the sea, yet they had never cried out.

Their lives were good in Chiniak. In the morning, they
might watch the sunrise with their relatives, sitting on the
sod roof of the big family house. During the day, when
they were not out gathering food on the land or on the
ocean in their two-person kayak, they might sit in the
large common room by the hearth. Or they might take
sweat baths in one of the small rooms attached to the
common room, where steam would rise as they placed
water on the heated stones. But whatever those cousins
did, they always did it together.

Those two girls had reached the age when they could

choose a husband. Both of them had just been given the chin tattoos that showed they were now women. Both of them were strong and good-looking, and they were so well liked that almost any young man would have agreed to marry them. In fact, some elders said that these girls might easily choose—as did some of the women—to each have two husbands. Yet none of the young men in the village of Chiniak or any of the other villages on the island or even the nearby mainland interested those cousins.

When the night had come and the work of the day was done, those two girls would always go down to the beach to play together in the sand and watch for the rising of the Moon above the water. As soon as he began to show his face, they would turn over their kayak and sit, leaning back against it, admiring the moon's beauty. They spent all their time at night staring at the sky. Whether it was winter or summer, they could always be found there at the beach.

One night, one of the girls said, "I have fallen in love with the Moon."

"I have fallen in love with the Moon, too," said the other girl. "If he ever comes down to the earth, I will marry him."

Their parents worried about them when they heard that the two girls wished to marry the Moon. But no one told them to stop going to the beach at night.

As they watched the Moon crossing the sky one night, it disappeared behind some heavy clouds.

"Why does the Moon have to hide his face so early in the night?" one cousin complained.

"Yes," said the other cousin, "I wish he would show himself again. I wish he would come here and choose one of us to marry him."

Suddenly they heard the sound of footsteps on the gravel of the beach and the voice of a young man.

"You have been saying that you love me," the voice said. "I have come to marry you."

The two girls leaped to their feet. A tall, handsome man wearing a beautiful mask on his face stood before them. That mask shone brightly, and they knew they were looking at the Moon.

"Yes," said the girls. "We will marry you."

"My work is hard," Moon said, "and I can take only one wife. I will take the one who is the most patient."

"We have always done everything together," said the girls. "You must take us both."

"Then you must close your eyes," Moon said. "Do not open them until I tell you."

The girls closed their eyes and waited. Moon reached down and held each of them by the long hair on her head, lifting them up into the air. The two cousins felt their feet leave the ground and they felt the wind whistling by them. They kept their eyes closed as they had been told, but when a long time had passed, one of the girls became impatient.

I must see where we are going, she thought. I will just open one eye a little.

But as soon as she opened her eye, she found herself falling down and landing back on the beach alone. Her long hair was gone from her head, and her cousin was gone from her forever.

The other girl, though, did not open her eyes. All through the night, she kept her eyes closed as Moon crossed the sky. When he told her to open her eyes at last, she found herself standing in Moon's house on the other side of the sky.

At first she was happy to be the wife of Moon.

"Go wherever you wish," her husband told her. "Only do not look behind the blanket and go into my storehouse."

Moon's wife agreed. She would do as her husband said. She settled down to her new life in the land on the other side of the sky, but it was not always easy. Sometimes her husband would spend a long time with her. Sometimes he would be gone all night and then sleep all day after he came home. She never knew when he was going to go or how long he would be gone. Soon she became bored.

"Why must you always leave me?" she said to her husband. "Why is it that you come and go in such a strange way?"

"It is the work I must do," said Moon. "That is why I cannot always be with you."

"Can I go with you when you do your work?"

"No," said Moon, "my work is too hard. You must stay home and be happy when I am with you."

Moon's wife listened, but she was not happy. That night when her husband left, she began to wander about the land on the other side of the sky. She walked farther and farther and came to a place where she saw many trails, and she began to follow one. At the end of that trail, she saw a person lying facedown.

"What are you doing?" she asked. But the person would not answer her or look her way.

She tried more trails and found the same thing at the end—a person lying facedown. And each time she asked what the person was doing, she received no answer. At last she could stand it no longer. At the end of the next trail she took, when she found a person lying down, she began to poke the person with her foot.

"Answer me," she said. "Answer me, answer me. What are you doing?"

Finally that person turned and looked at her. She saw he had only one bright eye, sparkling in the middle of his face. "I am working," the person said. "Do not bother me."

When Moon's wife returned home, her husband had not come back. She sat down to wait, but she was still bored. She looked around and saw his storeroom, with a dark woven blanket covering the door.

"It will not hurt to take one small look," she said. "Moon is my husband, and I should be able to go wherever I want in our house."

Then she went to the door and pulled aside the blanket. There in the storeroom were the pieces of light her husband wore when he crossed the sky. There was a half-moon, a quarter moon, and all the other phases. The only one missing was the full moon, which her husband had worn when he left that evening. The pieces of light were so beautiful that Moon's wife could not resist.

"I must try on one of them," she said, "to see how my husband feels when he is carrying them across the sky."

She reached down and picked up the one that was

almost full and placed it on her face. As soon as she did
so, it stuck there. She tried to remove it, but it would not
budge. Although she wept and cried, the piece of moon
would not come off. Then she heard her husband's steps
coming across the sky.

She climbed into their bed and covered her head with
a blanket.

"What is wrong?" Moon asked.

"I have a pain on my face," said his wife. "I do not
feel well. Leave me alone."

But Moon became suspicious. He went to his
storeroom and saw that one of the pieces of light was
gone. He went back to his wife and pulled the covers
from her head.

"Husband," Moon's wife said, "I became bored while
you were gone. I tried on this piece of moon and now it
is stuck."

Then Moon laughed. He laughed and laughed. And
with careful hands, he pulled that piece of moon from
her face.

"What else have you done today?" Moon said, still
laughing.

His wife told him about following the many trails that
led to people lying with their faces down and with a
single bright eye in each of their heads.

"Those people are the stars," Moon said. "They should
not be bothered while they are doing their work. It is
clear to me that you need work to do also, my wife.
Since you have shown that you are able to carry the
moon you can help me. From now on, I will carry the
pieces of moon each cycle until it is full, and then you

can carry the pieces of moon until it is dark. That way, we will both have time to rest and neither of us will grow bored."

So it is to this day. The man of the moon carries the pieces of light from the time of the moon's first quarter until it is full, and the woman of the moon carries them from the time it is full until the moon grows dark. So they share the duty of carrying light across the night sky.

AFTERWORD

A collection of traditional stories is almost never the sole product of the people named as authors, and this book is no exception. I owe a debt of love and gratitude to many people who guided me as I wrote the stories offered here.

Years ago an elderly Cherokee woman living in Canada sent me "Stonecoat" through my adopted brother, Chippewa-Cree storyteller Ron Evans. Ron brought the story to me with great care, recognizing the gift that it was. Chickasaw storyteller Bob Perry introduced me to "The Girl Who Married an Osage" and sent me a written version authorized by the Peoria people in Oklahoma. My beloved friend Teresa Pijoan was invaluable in guiding me through the many published versions of "The Poor Turkey Girl" and "The Girl Who Gave Birth to Water-Jar Boy." Two Navajo friends, dancer Jones Benally and storyteller Geri Keams, gave me insight into the character of "The Bear Woman." Karen Standifer Polachek spent hours patiently recounting every detail she could remember of the recent Beauty Way ceremony she attended on the Mescalero Apache Reservation in New Mexico. The list goes on and on.

The most important person to acknowledge, though, is my dear friend and collaborator, Joseph Bruchac. He was responsible for inviting me to become involved in this

project, and his support and encouragement gave me the much-needed courage to accept. The opportunity to work with Joe was exciting. He and I have been taught that stories are living spirits and that the role of the storyteller is to care for the tales in our keeping. It is my fervent hope that I have rendered these with the respect they deserve.

As I write, I keep before me the memory of my grandmother, Anne Ross Piburn, and the face of my daughter, Sarah Elizabeth Holt. I know that Sarah's life may be very different from my own; as mine is different from my grandmother's. In this changing world, with the roles of men and women being constantly redefined, I believe it is important that our definitions be based on mutual respect and the acceptance of our common humanity, our place in the circle of all living things. The stories are the teachers. May their spirits travel with you.

Gayle Ross

ACKNOWLEDGMENTS

Arrowhead Finger   The story of the brave young woman taken captive is a common motif in the stories of the Northeast. Published versions often contain only the second half of this story, "The Origin of Medicines." A brief telling may be found in Frank Speck's *Penobscot Tales*.

The Abandoned Girl   The story of the young woman rescued by the river serpent is found in Mohegan traditions from the Hudson River and Seneca traditions from the Niagara. A story similar to this was collected by Arthur Parker in *Seneca Myths and Legends*.

The Girl and the Chenoo   I've heard several versions of this story over the years, from both Abenaki traditions and the Iroquois, where the Chenoo is replaced by the Stone Giant. Other published versions can be found in Horace Beck's *Gluskap, The Liar* and Charles G. Leland's *Algonquin Legends*.

The Girl Who Escaped   I'm grateful to Mohegan elder Gladys Tantaquidgeon for the work she has done preserving the traditions of her people and for her generosity in sharing them. The retelling in this volume draws on both Mohegan traditions and similar tales told by the Western Abenaki.

The Girl Who Married the Moon   I first heard this story while visiting Alaska five years ago. A version of this story appeared in 1907, in the *Journal of American Folklore,* collected by Golder. Another version of this story may be found in *Voices of the Wind,* by Margot Edmonds and Ella E. Clark (*Facts on File,* 1989).

How Pelican Girl Was Saved   It's important to credit Malcolm Margolin—and his work with Heyday Press and the magazine *News From Native California*—for deepening my understanding (and that of many others) of the diversity and wonder of the many Native traditions of California. Wintu poet and painter Frank LaPena has just published a marvelous collection of Miwok Yosemite Indian Stories with Yosemite Association Press. Another written version of this story may be found in *California Indian Nights.*

Where The Girl Rescued Her Brother   I first heard of Buffalo Calf Road Woman many years ago from the Cheyenne poet Lance Henson, but was reminded of her again in recent years by Abenaki storyteller Wolf Song, who tells a wonderful version of this true exploit. My telling draws on a number of oral and written sources, including a brief version of the story to be found in John Neihardt's *Black Elk Speaks.*

Chipmunk Girl and Owl Woman   I was given permission to tell a version in English of this story by Okanagan writer and storyteller Jeanette Armstrong, who has been entrusted by her people with this particular tale. My version is modeled after a written telling done by her aunt, Mourning Dove, in her book *Coyote Tales.* Jay Silverheels recorded a version of this story on his Caedmon tape *Indian Wisdom Stories.*

Joseph Bruchac

SOURCES

Bruchac, Joseph. *Iroquois Stories*. Freedom: The Crossing Press, 1985.

Edoes, Richard and Alfonso Ortiz, eds. *American Indian Myths and Legends*. New York: Pantheon Books, 1984.

Gifford, Edward W. and Gweldoline Harris Block, *California Indian Nights*. Lincoln: University of Nebraska Press, 1990.

Lankford, George F. *Native American Legends (Southeastern Legends)*. Little Rock: August House Press, 1987.

Mourning Dove. *Coyote Stories*. Lincoln: University of Nebraska Press, 1990.

Parker, Arthur C. *Seneca Myths and Folktales*. Lincoln: University of Nebraska Press, 1989.

Pijoan, Teresa. *Healers on the Mountain*. Little Rock: August House Press, 1993.

Ross, Gayle. *How Rabbit Tricked Otter (and Other Cherokee Stories)*. New York: HarperCollins, 1994.